HOW MACHINES WORK

First published in 1976
Usborne Publishing Ltd
20 Garrick Street
London WC2E 9BJ
© Usborne Publishing Ltd 1976

The name Usborne and the device are
Trade Marks of Usborne Publishing Ltd.

Printed in Belgium by Henri Proost
Turnhout, Belgium.

We wish to thank the following
organizations for their help in
checking the material in this book.

Agricultural Press
Alfa-Laval
American Hoist and Derrick
Atlas Copco
Blackwood Hodge
British Aircraft Corp.
British Hovercraft Corp.
British Petroleum
British Rail
BSP International Foundations
Chubb Fire Security
Comex John Brown
Cunard-Trafalgar
ERF
GEC Machines
Hawker Siddeley Aviation
Hovercraft Development
Ing. Alfred Schmidt GMBH
Interconair
Lockheed Aircraft
Lola Cars
Massey Ferguson
Mining Magazine
Ministry of Defence
National Coal Board
Orenstein & Koppel
Plant Hire Magazine
Railway Gazette International
RNLI
Shipping World & Shipbuilder
Simon Engineering
Swiss National Tourist Office
Tarmac Construction
Vickers Oceanics
Westland Helicopters
Winget

About This Book

This book is a simple introduction to the world of machines and motors. It looks right inside lots of exciting modern machines and answers the questions 'How do they work?' and 'What do they do?'.

Here are machines which help us to farm, like the combine harvester and mining machines, like the bucket wheel excavator. You will see what happens on an oil rig and find out how a hovercraft floats on a cushion of air.

Join the Apollo astronauts as they circle high above the surface of the moon. Peep into the eerie world of a mini submarine deep underwater on the sea bed. This book will help you to understand the working of some of the most amazing machines in the world.

On pages 42–45 you will find lots of simple diagrams. They explain the motors which drive all the machines in the book, from the simple steam engine to the powerful rocket motor.

HOW MACHINES WORK

Christopher Rawson

Illustrated by Colin King

CONTENTS

4	Space Machines	28	Building Machines
6	Flying Machines	30	Road Making
8	Hovercraft	32	Mining and Excavating
10	Hovering Machines	34	Oil from under the Sea
12	Floating Machines	36	Farming Machines
14	Machines on Rails	38	Dairy Machines
16	Racing Machines	40	Home Machines
18	Underwater Machines	42	How Motors Work
20	Fighting Machines on Land	44	How Motors Work
22	Fighting Machines in the Air	46	Index
24	Fighting Machines at Sea	47	Picture Index
26	Rescue Machines		

Space Machines

Rockets need very powerful motors to blast them into space. This is because they have to overcome the pull of gravity—the force that holds everything down on the earth. Rockets carry astronauts into space and launch unmanned satellites to explore other planets.

ESCAPE TOWER
COMMAND MODULE
SERVICE MODULE
LUNAR MODULE IN HERE

ASTRONAUTS IN THE NOSE CONE

THIRD STAGE

GANTRY TO HOLD THE ROCKET STEADY

SECOND STAGE

FIRST STAGE

MAIN LAUNCH MOTORS

Saturn Blast-Off

The giant rocket fires its main engines. Astronauts in the nose cone set out for space from Cape Kennedy.

TANKS IN HERE CARRY ROCKET FUEL AND OXYGEN.

SERVICE MODULE

SERVICE MODULE ENGINES IN HERE ARE FIRED TO MAKE THE MOONCRAFT SLOW DOWN AND TO BRING IT BACK TO EARTH. SEE HOW A ROCKET MOTOR WORKS ON PAGE 43.

EXHAUST NOZZLE

THIS AERIAL PICKS UP RADIO SIGNALS FROM EARTH.

1 Viking

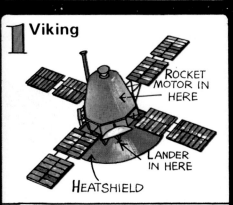

ROCKET MOTOR IN HERE

LANDER IN HERE

HEATSHIELD

This spacecraft was launched towards Mars in 1975. The journey took nearly a year. Inside the spacecraft, protected by the heat shield, was a fully automatic lander.

2

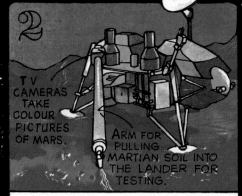

TV CAMERAS TAKE COLOUR PICTURES OF MARS.

ARM FOR PULLING MARTIAN SOIL INTO THE LANDER FOR TESTING.

The spacecraft released the lander while circling round Mars. The lander was fitted with cameras and many instruments to show scientists on earth what the surface of Mars is like.

Weather Satellite

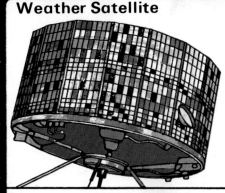

This sort of satellite stays in orbit round the earth for many years. Cameras inside it take pictures of the earth's surface. They warn scientists of bad weather, such as cyclones and tornadoes.

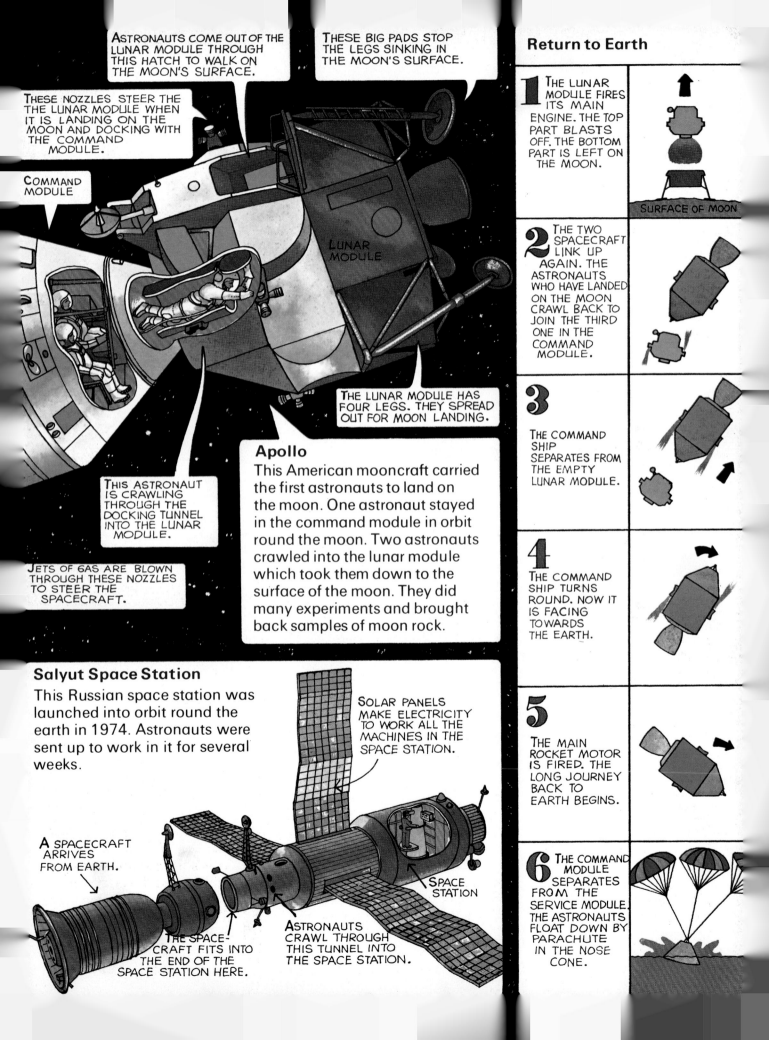

ASTRONAUTS COME OUT OF THE LUNAR MODULE THROUGH THIS HATCH TO WALK ON THE MOON'S SURFACE.

THESE BIG PADS STOP THE LEGS SINKING IN THE MOON'S SURFACE.

THESE NOZZLES STEER THE THE LUNAR MODULE WHEN IT IS LANDING ON THE MOON AND DOCKING WITH THE COMMAND MODULE.

COMMAND MODULE

LUNAR MODULE

THIS ASTRONAUT IS CRAWLING THROUGH THE DOCKING TUNNEL INTO THE LUNAR MODULE.

THE LUNAR MODULE HAS FOUR LEGS. THEY SPREAD OUT FOR MOON LANDING.

JETS OF GAS ARE BLOWN THROUGH THESE NOZZLES TO STEER THE SPACECRAFT.

Apollo

This American mooncraft carried the first astronauts to land on the moon. One astronaut stayed in the command module in orbit round the moon. Two astronauts crawled into the lunar module which took them down to the surface of the moon. They did many experiments and brought back samples of moon rock.

Salyut Space Station

This Russian space station was launched into orbit round the earth in 1974. Astronauts were sent up to work in it for several weeks.

SOLAR PANELS MAKE ELECTRICITY TO WORK ALL THE MACHINES IN THE SPACE STATION.

A SPACECRAFT ARRIVES FROM EARTH.

SPACE STATION

THE SPACE-CRAFT FITS INTO THE END OF THE SPACE STATION HERE.

ASTRONAUTS CRAWL THROUGH THIS TUNNEL INTO THE SPACE STATION.

Return to Earth

1 THE LUNAR MODULE FIRES ITS MAIN ENGINE. THE TOP PART BLASTS OFF. THE BOTTOM PART IS LEFT ON THE MOON.

SURFACE OF MOON

2 THE TWO SPACECRAFT LINK UP AGAIN. THE ASTRONAUTS WHO HAVE LANDED ON THE MOON CRAWL BACK TO JOIN THE THIRD ONE IN THE COMMAND MODULE.

3 THE COMMAND SHIP SEPARATES FROM THE EMPTY LUNAR MODULE.

4 THE COMMAND SHIP TURNS ROUND. NOW IT IS FACING TOWARDS THE EARTH.

5 THE MAIN ROCKET MOTOR IS FIRED. THE LONG JOURNEY BACK TO EARTH BEGINS.

6 THE COMMAND MODULE SEPARATES FROM THE SERVICE MODULE. THE ASTRONAUTS FLOAT DOWN BY PARACHUTE IN THE NOSE CONE.

Flying Machines

Aeroplanes fly through the air because their engines push them along and their wings keep them up in the air.

Aeroplanes can only leave the ground when air is rushing past their wings. They race down the runway to make this happen. Wings are flat underneath and curved on top. This makes the air go faster over the top. The air underneath pushes up and helps the plane to rise.

1 How Wings Work
HOLD A THIN SHEET OF PAPER BY THE CORNERS LIKE THIS.

2 BLOW HARD ACROSS THE TOP OF THE PAPER. THE AIR IS BLOWN AWAY. THE AIR BELOW PUSHES THE PAPER UP.

AIR PASSING OVER THE WINGS LETS THE PLANE RISE.

AIR BELOW PUSHES UP.

CONCORDE HAS SPECIAL FLAPS ON THE WINGS CALLED ELEVONS. THE PILOT MOVES THEM UP OR DOWN TO MAKE THE PLANE CLIMB OR DIVE. CONCORDE HAS ELEVONS BECAUSE IT DOES NOT HAVE A TAIL PLANE WITH ELEVATORS ON IT.

THE PILOT MOVES THE RUDDER TO TURN CONCORDE TO LEFT OR RIGHT.

THE TAIL WHEEL IS LOWERED FOR TAKE-OFF AND LANDING.

CONCORDE HAS FOUR TURBO-JET ENGINES LIKE THESE. TURN TO PAGE 42 TO SEE HOW JET ENGINE WORK.

THESE REVERSE THRUST BUCKETS CLOSE OVER THE BACK OF THE ENGINE AFTER LANDING. THEY HELP THE BRAKES TO STOP CONCORDE.

AFTER-BURNERS ARE BOOSTER MOTORS FITTED ON THE END OF THE JET ENGINES. THEY MAKE THE ENGINES MORE POWERFUL FOR TAKE-OFF AND GOING THROUGH THE SOUND BARRIER.

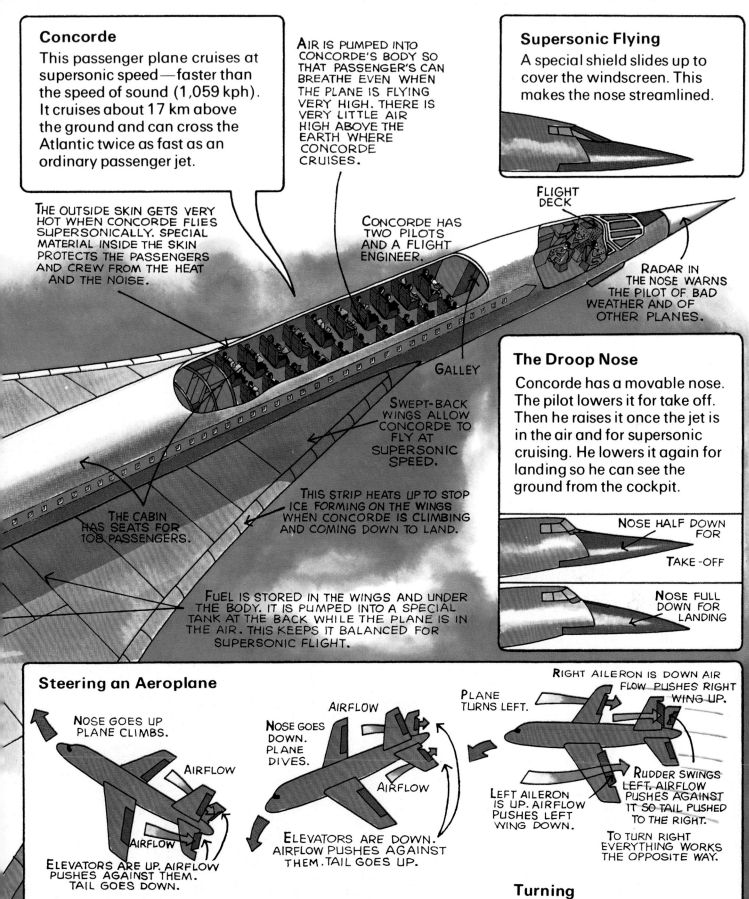

Concorde

This passenger plane cruises at supersonic speed—faster than the speed of sound (1,059 kph). It cruises about 17 km above the ground and can cross the Atlantic twice as fast as an ordinary passenger jet.

AIR IS PUMPED INTO CONCORDE'S BODY SO THAT PASSENGER'S CAN BREATHE EVEN WHEN THE PLANE IS FLYING VERY HIGH. THERE IS VERY LITTLE AIR HIGH ABOVE THE EARTH WHERE CONCORDE CRUISES.

Supersonic Flying

A special shield slides up to cover the windscreen. This makes the nose streamlined.

THE OUTSIDE SKIN GETS VERY HOT WHEN CONCORDE FLIES SUPERSONICALLY. SPECIAL MATERIAL INSIDE THE SKIN PROTECTS THE PASSENGERS AND CREW FROM THE HEAT AND THE NOISE.

CONCORDE HAS TWO PILOTS AND A FLIGHT ENGINEER.

FLIGHT DECK

RADAR IN THE NOSE WARNS THE PILOT OF BAD WEATHER AND OF OTHER PLANES.

GALLEY

SWEPT-BACK WINGS ALLOW CONCORDE TO FLY AT SUPERSONIC SPEED.

The Droop Nose

Concorde has a movable nose. The pilot lowers it for take off. Then he raises it once the jet is in the air and for supersonic cruising. He lowers it again for landing so he can see the ground from the cockpit.

NOSE HALF DOWN FOR TAKE-OFF

NOSE FULL DOWN FOR LANDING

THE CABIN HAS SEATS FOR 108 PASSENGERS.

THIS STRIP HEATS UP TO STOP ICE FORMING ON THE WINGS WHEN CONCORDE IS CLIMBING AND COMING DOWN TO LAND.

FUEL IS STORED IN THE WINGS AND UNDER THE BODY. IT IS PUMPED INTO A SPECIAL TANK AT THE BACK WHILE THE PLANE IS IN THE AIR. THIS KEEPS IT BALANCED FOR SUPERSONIC FLIGHT.

Steering an Aeroplane

NOSE GOES UP PLANE CLIMBS.

AIRFLOW

AIRFLOW

ELEVATORS ARE UP. AIRFLOW PUSHES AGAINST THEM. TAIL GOES DOWN.

NOSE GOES DOWN. PLANE DIVES.

AIRFLOW

AIRFLOW

ELEVATORS ARE DOWN. AIRFLOW PUSHES AGAINST THEM. TAIL GOES UP.

PLANE TURNS LEFT.

RIGHT AILERON IS DOWN AIR FLOW PUSHES RIGHT WING UP.

LEFT AILERON IS UP. AIRFLOW PUSHES LEFT WING DOWN.

RUDDER SWINGS LEFT. AIRFLOW PUSHES AGAINST IT SO TAIL PUSHED TO THE RIGHT.

TO TURN RIGHT EVERYTHING WORKS THE OPPOSITE WAY.

Climbing

The pilot raises flaps, called elevators, on the tail. They make the plane climb.

Diving

He lowers the elevators to make the plane dive.

Turning

The pilot moves the rudder on the tail to turn the plane. Flaps on the wings called ailerons make it bank.

7

Hovercraft

Hovercraft can travel over water, ice, mud and any flat land. They skim along, just above the surface, on a cushion of air.

This SRN4 hovercraft can carry 254 passengers and 30 cars. It goes at speeds of up to 130 kph. and rides over waves up to 3 metres high.

How a Hovercraft Works

Fans suck in air at the top and blow it out underneath the skirt. The hovercraft rises up on the air trapped by the skirt.

The propellers start to turn. When they grip the air, they push the hovercraft along.

When the engines are switched off, the hovercraft stops. The fans stop pushing air down into the skirt and the hovercraft sinks slowly down to rest on its base.

The propellers push the hovercraft along. The angles of the blades are changed to move it forwards slowly or very fast, or backwards.

The propellers can move round on their posts. They swing to the left to turn the hovercraft to the right. They swing right to turn it left.

INNER CABIN

CAPTAIN'S CABIN

ANCHOR

LIFEBOATS

The rubber skirt holds in the cushion of air. This cushion is about 2.5 metres deep.

The skirt bulges out at the top to stop the hovercraft from rolling from side to side.

The flaps on these big fins can be moved from side to side. The captain uses them to change course.

Four big gas turbine engines turn the fans to lift the hovercraft off the ground. They also turn the propellers which push the hovercraft along.

In Canada, some rivers freeze over in winter. This Voyageur hovercraft is breaking up the ice. Its cushion of air pushes down on it and cracks ice up to 1 metre thick.

CAR DECK

AIR GOES IN HERE

PASSENGER DOOR

In 1968 this small hovercraft travelled over 3,000 kilometres of dangerous rivers and rapids in South America.

There are four fans, one under each propeller. The fans are 3.5 metres across. Each one has twelve blades. The fans suck in air to push the hovercraft up off the ground or the water.

The bottom of the skirt moves up and down, following the shape of the waves. This keeps the hovercraft steady.

This huge oil tank weighs 630 tonnes. Workmen can move it easily on a cushion of air, just like a hovercraft.

Hovering Machines

The two planes on these pages can fly along, up and down and hover in the air. The Harrier jet fighter can take off from small secret bases and from ships at sea.

Helicopters are useful for getting to places where there are no proper landing fields or roads.

Firing Missiles

The Harrier is firing one of its air-to-ground rockets. It can carry 2,270 kgs. of weapons under its body and wings.

Mid-air Refuelling

The Harrier pilot steers his probe into the funnel on the end of the fuel pipe. Jet fuel is then pumped from the tanker plane.

In the cockpit, a moving map on a screen tells the pilot about the ground below. A display on the windscreen helps him to fire his weapons accurately.

These flaps are for steering. Turn to page 6 to see how a pilot steers his aircraft.

The Harrier can fly at 1,186 kph. The jet engine sucks in air through a hole in each side. Turn to page 42 to see how different jet engines work.

Exhaust gases from the engine blow out through nozzles. When the nozzles point down the thrust of the engine lifts the plane up. When they point back, the plane goes forward.

The small propeller at the back stops the helicopter spinning round when the big blades are turning.

This helicopter has two gas turbine engines. This means it can still fly even if one engine fails. These engines turn the main blades and the small propeller at the back.

These big blades whirl round very fast. They push the air down. This keeps the helicopter up in the air. It is hovering. The pictures at the bottom of the page show how a helicopter flies up and along.

This helicopter is rescuing injured people. It can carry three stretchers and two doctors in the cabin.

The winch lifts people up when the helicopter cannot land. It can lift two people at a time.

How a Helicopter Flies

BLADES FLAT. HELICOPTER STAYS ON THE GROUND.

The pilot starts the motor. The big blades spin round but the helicopter stays still on the ground.

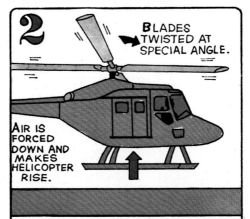

2

BLADES TWISTED AT SPECIAL ANGLE.

AIR IS FORCED DOWN AND MAKES HELICOPTER RISE.

When the pilot makes the big blades twist at an angle, they grip the air. Then the helicopter rises off the ground.

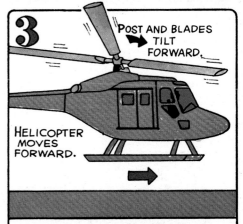

3

POST AND BLADES TILT FORWARD.

HELICOPTER MOVES FORWARD.

Then the pilot tilts the blades forward. The helicopter stops rising and moves along.

Floating Machines

These pictures show some of the different things that ships are used for at sea. Ships cannot travel as fast as aeroplanes or many vehicles on land, but they can carry very large and heavy cargoes over long distances.

EXHAUST GASES FROM THE DIESEL ENGINES ARE BLOWN OUT THROUGH THE FUNNEL.

Steering a Ship

Ships have propellers to push them along. They are steered by turning the rudder at the end of the ship to one side or the other.

SHIP SAILS STRAIGHT AHEAD.
RUDDER IS STRAIGHT.

SHIP TURNS LEFT.
RUDDER IS MOVED TO THE LEFT.

SHIP TURNS RIGHT.
RUDDER IS TURNED TO THE RIGHT.

Some ships have two engines and two propellers. These ships can be turned sharply by keeping one propeller going forwards, putting the other into reverse, and changing the angle of the rudder.

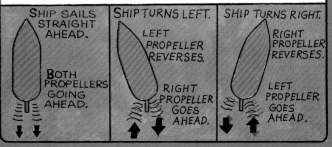

SHIP SAILS STRAIGHT AHEAD.
BOTH PROPELLERS GOING AHEAD.

SHIP TURNS LEFT.
LEFT PROPELLER REVERSES.
RIGHT PROPELLER GOES AHEAD.

SHIP TURNS RIGHT.
RIGHT PROPELLER REVERSES.
LEFT PROPELLER GOES AHEAD.

ALL BIG SHIPS CARRY LIFE BOATS. PASSENGERS AND CREW USE THEM TO ESCAPE IN EMERGENCY.

THE BACK OF A SHIP IS CALLED THE STERN

THE ENGINE ROOM IS JUST BELOW THE WATER LINE. THIS SHIP HAS TWO DIESEL ENGINES. SEE HOW DIESEL ENGINES WORK ON PAGE 45.

RUDDER

THE PROPELLERS ARE JOINED TO THE ENGINES BY LONG SHAFTS. AS THE PROPELLERS SPIN ROUND THEY TRY TO PUSH THE WATER BACKWARDS. THIS MOVES THE SHIP FORWARDS.

THE BOTTOM OF A SHIP IS CALLED THE KEEL. THIS KEEL IS 5·5 METRES BELOW THE WATER LINE. SOME SHIPS LIKE GIANT OIL TANKERS HAVE KEELS 60 METRES BELOW THE WATER LINE.

Dumping Log Carrier

This ship carries logs to a paper mill. Big water tanks inside the ship hold it steady when the logs slide off into the water.

1 CRANES ON THE SHIP LOAD THE LOGS.

2 THE SHIP CARRIES ITS LOAD. THE EXTRA WEIGHT PUSHES IT LOWER IN THE WATER.

3 TO UNLOAD, THE WATER IS PUMPED TO ONE SIDE. THE SHIP TILTS UNTIL THE LOGS FALL OFF.

4 WHEN THE LOGS FALL OFF, SOME OF THE WATER FLOWS BACK TO THE OTHER SIDE. THE SHIP RIGHTS ITSELF.

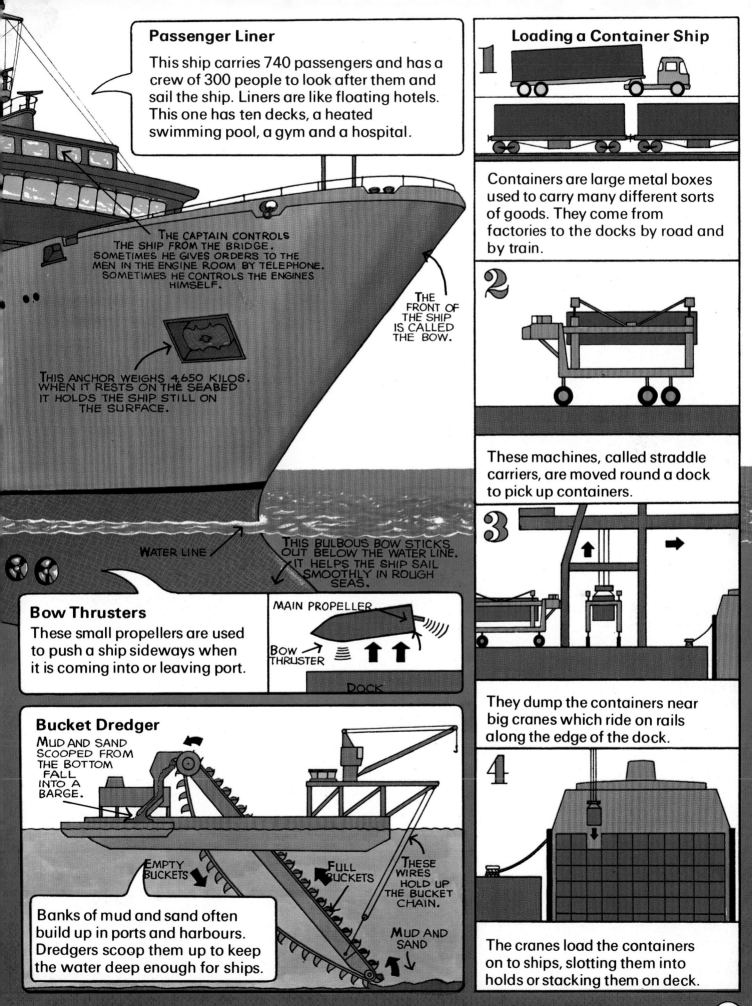

Passenger Liner

This ship carries 740 passengers and has a crew of 300 people to look after them and sail the ship. Liners are like floating hotels. This one has ten decks, a heated swimming pool, a gym and a hospital.

THE CAPTAIN CONTROLS THE SHIP FROM THE BRIDGE. SOMETIMES HE GIVES ORDERS TO THE MEN IN THE ENGINE ROOM BY TELEPHONE. SOMETIMES HE CONTROLS THE ENGINES HIMSELF.

THE FRONT OF THE SHIP IS CALLED THE BOW.

THIS ANCHOR WEIGHS 4,650 KILOS. WHEN IT RESTS ON THE SEABED IT HOLDS THE SHIP STILL ON THE SURFACE.

WATER LINE

THIS BULBOUS BOW STICKS OUT BELOW THE WATER LINE. IT HELPS THE SHIP SAIL SMOOTHLY IN ROUGH SEAS.

Bow Thrusters

These small propellers are used to push a ship sideways when it is coming into or leaving port.

MAIN PROPELLER

BOW THRUSTER

DOCK

Bucket Dredger

MUD AND SAND SCOOPED FROM THE BOTTOM FALL INTO A BARGE.

EMPTY BUCKETS

FULL BUCKETS

THESE WIRES HOLD UP THE BUCKET CHAIN.

MUD AND SAND

Banks of mud and sand often build up in ports and harbours. Dredgers scoop them up to keep the water deep enough for ships.

Loading a Container Ship

1

Containers are large metal boxes used to carry many different sorts of goods. They come from factories to the docks by road and by train.

2

These machines, called straddle carriers, are moved round a dock to pick up containers.

3

They dump the containers near big cranes which ride on rails along the edge of the dock.

4

The cranes load the containers on to ships, slotting them into holds or stacking them on deck.

Machines on Rails

Trains are used all over the world to carry goods and passengers. Modern electric and diesel engines are easier to run for long distances than the old steam engines. Turn to pages 42–45 to see how they all work.

Steam Engine

Steam engines need coal for the fire and water to fill the boiler. Together they make steam to turn the wheels.

How Wheels Fit the Rails

A ridge on the inside edge keeps the wheel from slipping off the rail.

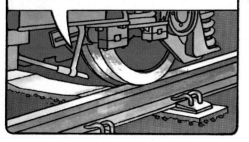

Underground Train

Some big cities, such as Paris, London and New York, have underground passenger railways. The engines are driven by electricity which is picked up from a third rail beside the track. The doors slide open sideways automatically to let the passengers off and on.

THIS CABLE CARRIES ELECTRICITY. IT IS HELD UP BY STEEL POSTS BESIDE THE TRACK.

THE CABLE HANGS FROM SPECIAL PIECES OF CHINA CALLED INSULATORS. THEY STOP THE ELECTRICITY GETTING INTO THE POSTS.

THE DRIVER CONTROLS THE ENGINE FROM HIS CAB. LOTS OF DIFFERENT DIALS SHOW HIM THAT ALL THE PARTS ARE WORKING PROPERLY.

Electric Train

This engine has four electric motors. It can get up speed very quickly, even when pulling a long, heavy train. The electricity which drives the motors is made at power stations and is carried by overhead cables.

Laying a New Line

When rails and sleepers are worn out, they are taken up and new ones laid in their place. First the new rail (red) is laid beside the old one (blue). Now follow the numbers in the picture to see how this machine picks up the old rails and lays down the new ones.

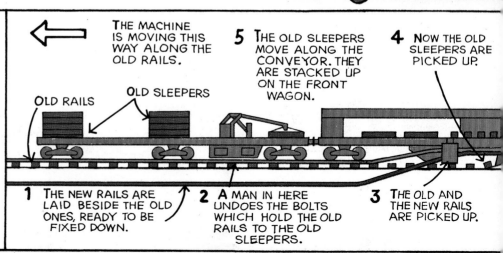

THE MACHINE IS MOVING THIS WAY ALONG THE OLD RAILS.

OLD RAILS

OLD SLEEPERS

5 THE OLD SLEEPERS MOVE ALONG THE CONVEYOR. THEY ARE STACKED UP ON THE FRONT WAGON.

4 NOW THE OLD SLEEPERS ARE PICKED UP.

1 THE NEW RAILS ARE LAID BESIDE THE OLD ONES, READY TO BE FIXED DOWN.

2 A MAN IN HERE UNDOES THE BOLTS WHICH HOLD THE OLD RAILS TO THE OLD SLEEPERS.

3 THE OLD AND THE NEW RAILS ARE PICKED UP.

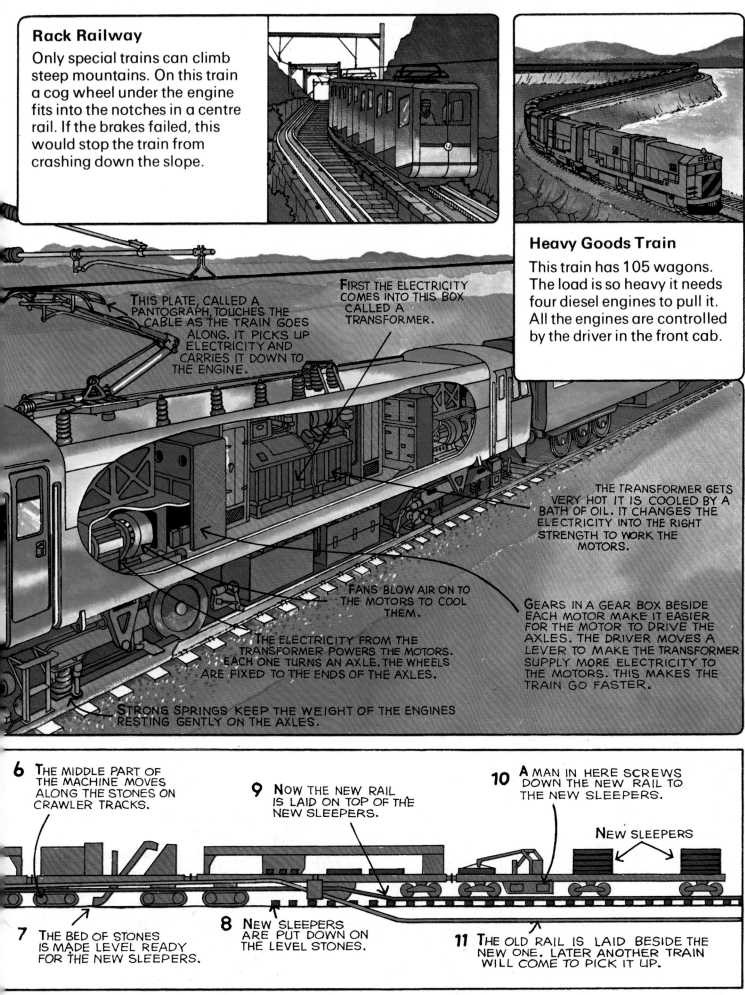

Rack Railway

Only special trains can climb steep mountains. On this train a cog wheel under the engine fits into the notches in a centre rail. If the brakes failed, this would stop the train from crashing down the slope.

Heavy Goods Train

This train has 105 wagons. The load is so heavy it needs four diesel engines to pull it. All the engines are controlled by the driver in the front cab.

THIS PLATE, CALLED A PANTOGRAPH, TOUCHES THE CABLE AS THE TRAIN GOES ALONG. IT PICKS UP ELECTRICITY AND CARRIES IT DOWN TO THE ENGINE.

FIRST THE ELECTRICITY COMES INTO THIS BOX CALLED A TRANSFORMER.

THE TRANSFORMER GETS VERY HOT IT IS COOLED BY A BATH OF OIL. IT CHANGES THE ELECTRICITY INTO THE RIGHT STRENGTH TO WORK THE MOTORS.

FANS BLOW AIR ON TO THE MOTORS TO COOL THEM.

THE ELECTRICITY FROM THE TRANSFORMER POWERS THE MOTORS. EACH ONE TURNS AN AXLE. THE WHEELS ARE FIXED TO THE ENDS OF THE AXLES.

GEARS IN A GEAR BOX BESIDE EACH MOTOR MAKE IT EASIER FOR THE MOTOR TO DRIVE THE AXLES. THE DRIVER MOVES A LEVER TO MAKE THE TRANSFORMER SUPPLY MORE ELECTRICITY TO THE MOTORS. THIS MAKES THE TRAIN GO FASTER.

STRONG SPRINGS KEEP THE WEIGHT OF THE ENGINES RESTING GENTLY ON THE AXLES.

6 THE MIDDLE PART OF THE MACHINE MOVES ALONG THE STONES ON CRAWLER TRACKS.

9 NOW THE NEW RAIL IS LAID ON TOP OF THE NEW SLEEPERS.

10 A MAN IN HERE SCREWS DOWN THE NEW RAIL TO THE NEW SLEEPERS.

NEW SLEEPERS

7 THE BED OF STONES IS MADE LEVEL READY FOR THE NEW SLEEPERS.

8 NEW SLEEPERS ARE PUT DOWN ON THE LEVEL STONES.

11 THE OLD RAIL IS LAID BESIDE THE NEW ONE. LATER ANOTHER TRAIN WILL COME TO PICK IT UP.

Racing Machines

All these machines are specially made for sport racing. Most of them are very light and have a powerful engine to push them along the ground or over water as fast as possible. All the ones which race on land also need very safe brakes to make them stop.

This ordinary car has been made extra strong and fast for long-distance races. Metal studs in the tyres stop it skidding on ice.

Racing Car

This picture shows some of the special parts which make a racing car different from an ordinary car. The body is pointed at the front so it cuts easily through the air. When the car is being raced, the petrol engine behind the driver uses a litre of petrol every 2.5 kilometres.

THIS RACING CAR HAS A PETROL ENGINE WITH EIGHT CYLINDERS. SEE WHAT HAPPENS INSIDE A PETROL ENGINE ON PAGE 44.

AIR BLOWS INTO THIS SCOOP. IT IS MIXED WITH THE PETROL IN THE ENGINE.

GEARS IN THE GEAR BOX MAKE THE ENGINE DRIVE THE BACK WHEELS FASTER OR SLOWER.

AS THE CAR RACES ALONG, THE AIR PUSHES AGAINST THIS WING. THIS PRESSES THE BACK WHEELS DOWN ON THE TRACK.

EXHAUST GASES FROM THE ENGINE ARE BLOWN OUT HERE.

THE BACK TYRES ARE VERY BIG AND SMOOTH SO THAT AS MUCH POWER AS POSSIBLE PUSHES AGAINST THE ROAD. THIS MAKES THE CAR GO FASTER.

OIL IN HERE IS PUMPED INTO THE MOTOR TO KEEP ALL THE DIFFERENT PARTS MOVING EASILY.

SPECIAL RUBBER BAGS IN THE SIDES OF THE CAR CONTAIN 118 LITRES OF PETROL. THE PETROL IS PUMPED FROM BOTH SIDES AT ONCE TO KEEP THE CAR BALANCED.

Changing Tyres in the Pits

When it rains during a race, mechanics fit special tyres with grooves to the cars to stop them skidding. All four tyres can be changed in 30 seconds.

Dragster

These cars race on short, straight tracks at speeds up to 380 kph. They go so fast that they have parachutes to help them stop at the end of a race.

Motor Cycle

These motor cycles race on roads or specially-curved tracks at up to 280 kph. Expert riders lean right over with their machines to go very fast round corners.

A RACING DRIVER WEARS A HELMET, GOGGLES AND A FLAME-PROOF SUIT TO PROTECT HIM IN CASE OF AN ACCIDENT.

A FIRE EXTINGUISHER UNDER THE DRIVER'S SEAT WILL SQUIRT AUTOMATICALLY ON TO THE DRIVER IF THE CAR BURSTS INTO FLAMES AFTER AN ACCIDENT. ANOTHER ONE SQUIRTS ON THE ENGINE.

RACING CARS DO NOT HAVE SPEEDOMETERS. A REV-COUNTER SHOWS THE DRIVER HOW MUCH WORK THE ENGINE IS DOING.

Power Boat

Racing boats are specially-shaped to skim over the water. When a boat is racing at full speed, it lifts up at the front until most of it is out of the water.

AIR BLOWS THROUGH SCOOPS ONTO THE BRAKES. IT KEEPS THEM COOL DURING A RACE.

WHEN THE DRIVER TURNS THE STEERING WHEEL, GEARS IN HERE TURN THE FRONT WHEELS.

THESE WINGS HELP TO KEEP THE FRONT TYRES ON THE TRACK. RACING CARS GO SO FAST THEY WOULD LIFT OFF THE GROUND WITHOUT THEM.

Finding a Lost Torpedo

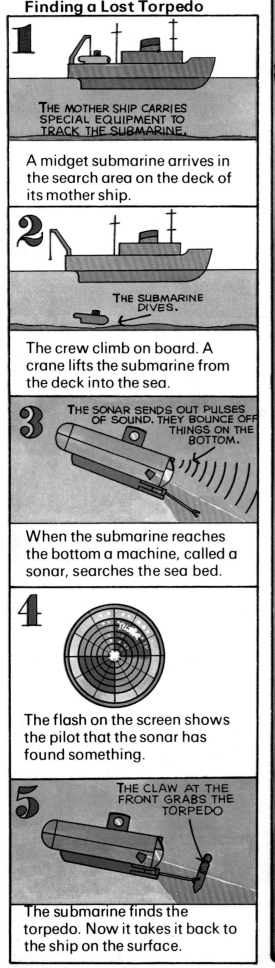

1

THE MOTHER SHIP CARRIES SPECIAL EQUIPMENT TO TRACK THE SUBMARINE.

A midget submarine arrives in the search area on the deck of its mother ship.

2

THE SUBMARINE DIVES.

The crew climb on board. A crane lifts the submarine from the deck into the sea.

3

THE SONAR SENDS OUT PULSES OF SOUND. THEY BOUNCE OFF THINGS ON THE BOTTOM.

When the submarine reaches the bottom a machine, called a sonar, searches the sea bed.

4

The flash on the screen shows the pilot that the sonar has found something.

5

THE CLAW AT THE FRONT GRABS THE TORPEDO

The submarine finds the torpedo. Now it takes it back to the ship on the surface.

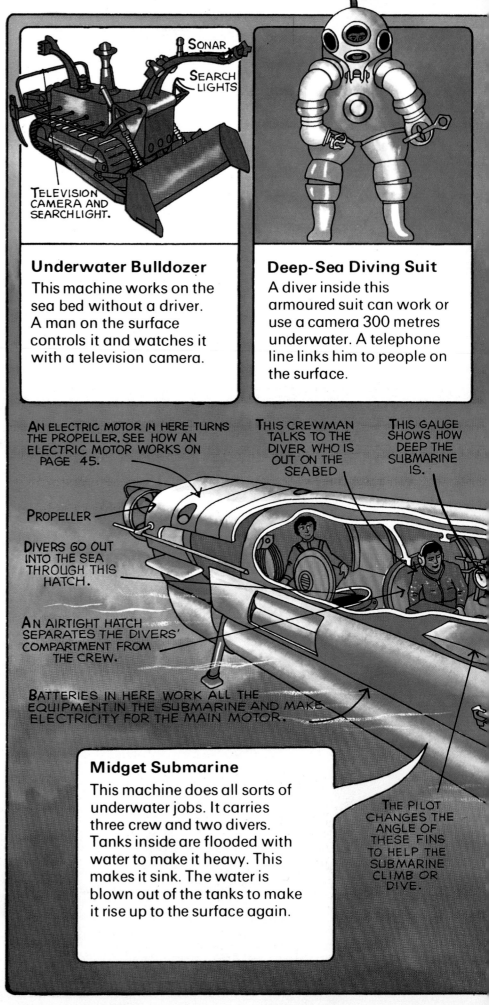

SONAR

SEARCH LIGHTS

TELEVISION CAMERA AND SEARCHLIGHT.

Underwater Bulldozer
This machine works on the sea bed without a driver. A man on the surface controls it and watches it with a television camera.

Deep-Sea Diving Suit
A diver inside this armoured suit can work or use a camera 300 metres underwater. A telephone line links him to people on the surface.

AN ELECTRIC MOTOR IN HERE TURNS THE PROPELLER. SEE HOW AN ELECTRIC MOTOR WORKS ON PAGE 45.

THIS CREWMAN TALKS TO THE DIVER WHO IS OUT ON THE SEABED

THIS GAUGE SHOWS HOW DEEP THE SUBMARINE IS.

PROPELLER

DIVERS GO OUT INTO THE SEA THROUGH THIS HATCH.

AN AIRTIGHT HATCH SEPARATES THE DIVERS' COMPARTMENT FROM THE CREW.

BATTERIES IN HERE WORK ALL THE EQUIPMENT IN THE SUBMARINE AND MAKE ELECTRICITY FOR THE MAIN MOTOR.

Midget Submarine
This machine does all sorts of underwater jobs. It carries three crew and two divers. Tanks inside are flooded with water to make it heavy. This makes it sink. The water is blown out of the tanks to make it rise up to the surface again.

THE PILOT CHANGES THE ANGLE OF THESE FINS TO HELP THE SUBMARINE CLIMB OR DIVE.

Underwater Machines

Many different machines are used to explore the sea bed and work underwater. The ones that dive very deep have to be a special shape and extra strong. This is to stop them being squashed by the huge weight of water pressing down on them.

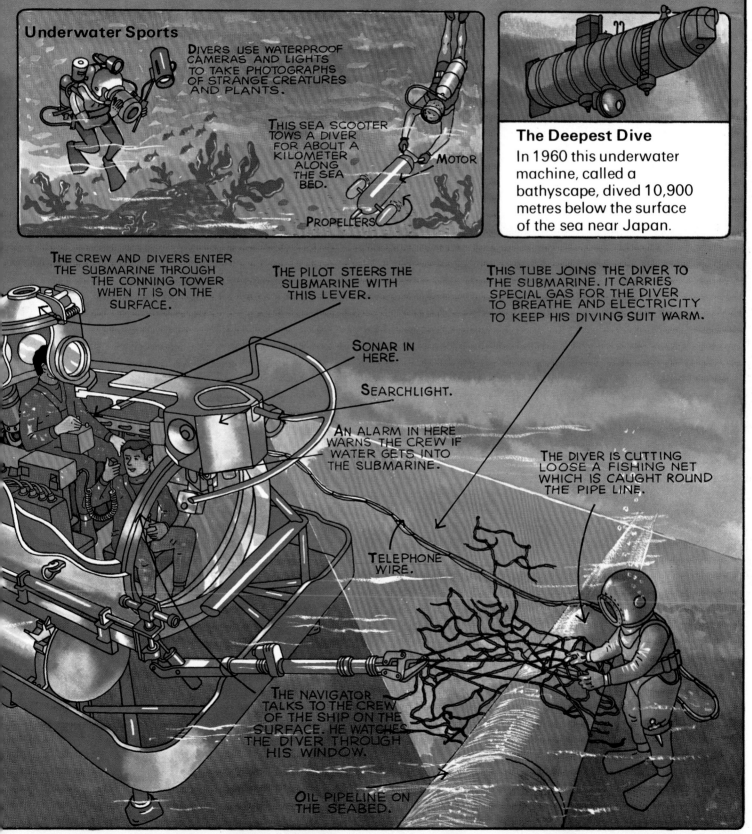

Underwater Sports

DIVERS USE WATERPROOF CAMERAS AND LIGHTS TO TAKE PHOTOGRAPHS OF STRANGE CREATURES AND PLANTS.

THIS SEA SCOOTER TOWS A DIVER FOR ABOUT A KILOMETER ALONG THE SEA BED.

MOTOR

PROPELLERS

The Deepest Dive
In 1960 this underwater machine, called a bathyscape, dived 10,900 metres below the surface of the sea near Japan.

THE CREW AND DIVERS ENTER THE SUBMARINE THROUGH THE CONNING TOWER WHEN IT IS ON THE SURFACE.

THE PILOT STEERS THE SUBMARINE WITH THIS LEVER.

THIS TUBE JOINS THE DIVER TO THE SUBMARINE. IT CARRIES SPECIAL GAS FOR THE DIVER TO BREATHE AND ELECTRICITY TO KEEP HIS DIVING SUIT WARM.

SONAR IN HERE.

SEARCHLIGHT.

AN ALARM IN HERE WARNS THE CREW IF WATER GETS INTO THE SUBMARINE.

THE DIVER IS CUTTING LOOSE A FISHING NET WHICH IS CAUGHT ROUND THE PIPE LINE.

TELEPHONE WIRE.

THE NAVIGATOR TALKS TO THE CREW OF THE SHIP ON THE SURFACE. HE WATCHES THE DIVER THROUGH HIS WINDOW.

OIL PIPELINE ON THE SEABED.

Fighting Machines on Land

Modern armies use tanks and armoured cars like the ones on these pages to fight battles on land.

They are made of thick steel plates to protect the soldiers inside from enemy bullets and mines.

The tank is painted in different colours to make it difficult to see. This is called camouflage.

Battle Tank

This fighting machine has a crew of four—a commander, a gunner, a driver and a radio operator. It has two diesel engines at the back. The main one turns the wheels which drive the crawler tracks round. The small one helps the main engine to start.

RADIO AERIAL

TANK COMMANDER

TANK COMMANDER'S MACHINE GUN

THIS SEARCHLIGHT SHINES SPECIAL RAYS, CALLED INFRA-RED RAYS, AT ENEMY TARGETS AT NIGHT. NO ONE CAN SEE THE RAYS. THE TARGET SHOWS UP ON A SCREEN INSIDE.

SMOKE GRENADES ARE FIRED FROM HERE.

THE WHOLE TURRET TURNS RIGHT ROUND SO THAT THE GUN CAN FIRE IN ALL DIRECTIONS.

SPARE AMMUNITION FOR THE MAIN GUN IS STORED IN SPECIAL BINS OF WATER INSIDE THE TANK TO PREVENT EXPLOSIONS.

ALL THE HATCHES, LIKE THIS ONE, MUST FIT VERY TIGHTLY TO STOP WATER AND FLAMES GETTING INTO THE TANK.

THE DRIVER SITS LOW AT THE FRONT. HE STEERS THE TANK BY MAKING THE WHEELS ON ONE SIDE GO FASTER THAN THE OTHER.

THE BOTTOM OF THE TANK IS ROUNDED TO MAKE IT EXTRA STRONG IN CASE A MINE EXPLODES UNDER IT.

1 **What a Tank Can Do**

TANKS ARE WATERTIGHT AND CAN CROSS RIVERS. THE COMMANDER GIVES ORDERS TO THE CREW FROM THE TOP OF THE TOWER.

COMMANDER'S WATERTIGHT TOWER

2 THE GROOVES IN THE STEEL TRACKS GRAB A STEEP BANK. THE TANK'S POWERFUL MOTOR PUSHES IT UP.

3 TANKS MAKE SMOKE SCREENS DURING A BATTLE TO HIDE THEIR EXACT POSITION FROM THE ENEMY.

Guided Missile

This weapon is fired from an armoured car. It trails very thin wires behind it as it flies through the air. The soldier in the armoured car guides it on to the target by steering it with the wires.

A MACHINE IN THE TAIL RECEIVES MESSAGES DOWN THE WIRES. IT GUIDES THE MISSILE THROUGH THE AIR.

THESE FINS POP OUT WHEN THE MISSILE LEAVES ITS TUBE.

CRUISING MOTOR

THE HEAD OF THE MISSILE IS FULL OF EXPLOSIVES.

RAPID MOTOR FOR LAUNCHING

1 THE MISSILE IS READY IN ITS TUBE.

The commander of the armoured car sights an enemy tank. The missile is in its tube.

2 FINS POP OUT.

WIRES TRAIL BEHIND.

He fires. The missile flies towards its target at 260 metres a second.

3 He scores a direct hit. The explosives in the nose of the missile blow up the tank.

THIS MAIN GUN FIRES SHELLS UP TO 5,000 METRES AWAY. A SPECIAL PART INSIDE THE TANK KEEPS IT AIMING AT ITS TARGET EVEN WHEN THE TANK IS MOVING OVER BUMPY GROUND.

Armoured Troop Carrier

This machine carries 12 soldiers into battle. It can travel at 80 kph on roads. It is watertight and can go over water. Sometimes the carrier is used as an ambulance —it has room for seven wounded soldiers and two doctors.

SOLDIERS INSIDE FIRE THEIR WEAPONS THROUGH SMALL WINDOWS AND SLITS IN THE BACK AND SIDES.

THE TYRES HAVE SPECIAL TUBES WHICH CANNOT BE PUNCTURED

STEEL TRACKS COVER THE WHEELS.

ALL THE WINDOWS ARE MADE OF VERY STRONG GLASS. THEY WILL NOT BREAK EVEN WHEN BULLETS HIT THEM.

THE BOTTOM IS HIGH OFF THE GROUND SO THE CARRIER CAN TRAVEL OVER VERY BUMPY GROUND.

4 POWERFUL SEARCHLIGHTS ALLOW TANKS TO MOVE AND FIRE AT ENEMY TARGETS AT NIGHT.

5 THIS TANK CARRIES A SPECIAL BRIDGE—FOLDED UP ON TOP OF ITS ROOF.

THE TANK COMMANDER STOPS AT A RIVER BANK, THE BRIDGE BEGINS TO UNFOLD.

WHEN THE BRIDGE IS LAID, THE TANK WITHDRAWS. NOW TROOPS AND OTHER VEHICLES CAN CROSS.

Fighting Machines in the Air

Fighting aeroplanes do many different jobs. Reconnaissance planes fly very high and fast to avoid enemy guns and missiles. Fighters are ready to attack enemy planes in the air, and transport planes carry troops and heavy weapons.

A WINDSOCK SHOWS WHICH WAY THE WIND IS BLOWING. THIS IS IMPORTANT BECAUSE PLANES TAKE OFF AND LAND MORE EASILY INTO THE WIND.

F.16 Fighter

This plane flies at over twice the speed of sound. It is very light and can turn quickly to dodge enemy planes during an air battle.

RADAR IN THE NOSE TRACKS ENEMY PLANES.

A RADAR SCREEN IN THE COCKPIT SHOWS THE PILOT WHICH WAY TO FLY.

COCKPIT COVER

AMMUNITION STORED HERE.

THIS BELT TAKES AMMUNITION TO THE GUN.

FLYING CONTROLS IN HERE.

GUN

THE PILOT PRESSES THIS PEDAL TO MOVE THE RUDDER.

THE ENGINE SUCKS IN AIR HERE.

AIR TUNNEL TO ENGINE.

FRONT LANDING WHEEL

SR.71A Blackbird

This reconnaissance plane cruises at 24,000 metres up, at three times the speed of sound. Special cameras, which can see through clouds, take photographs of the ground.

HATCH FOR MID-AIR REFUELLING.

THE TWO-MAN CREW WEAR SPACE SUITS TO PROTECT THEM IN CASE THEY HAVE TO EJECT AT GREAT HEIGHT.

MRCA Fighter

This plane has movable wings. The parts near the fuselage are fixed but the ends can swing backwards or forwards. When the wings are forward, the plane can take off and land slowly. When they are back, it cuts through the air more easily and can fly faster.

WINGS FORWARD FOR TAKING OFF AND LANDING.

WINGS BACK FOR SPEED.

ENGINE SUCKS IN AIR HERE.

NOSE LANDING WHEEL

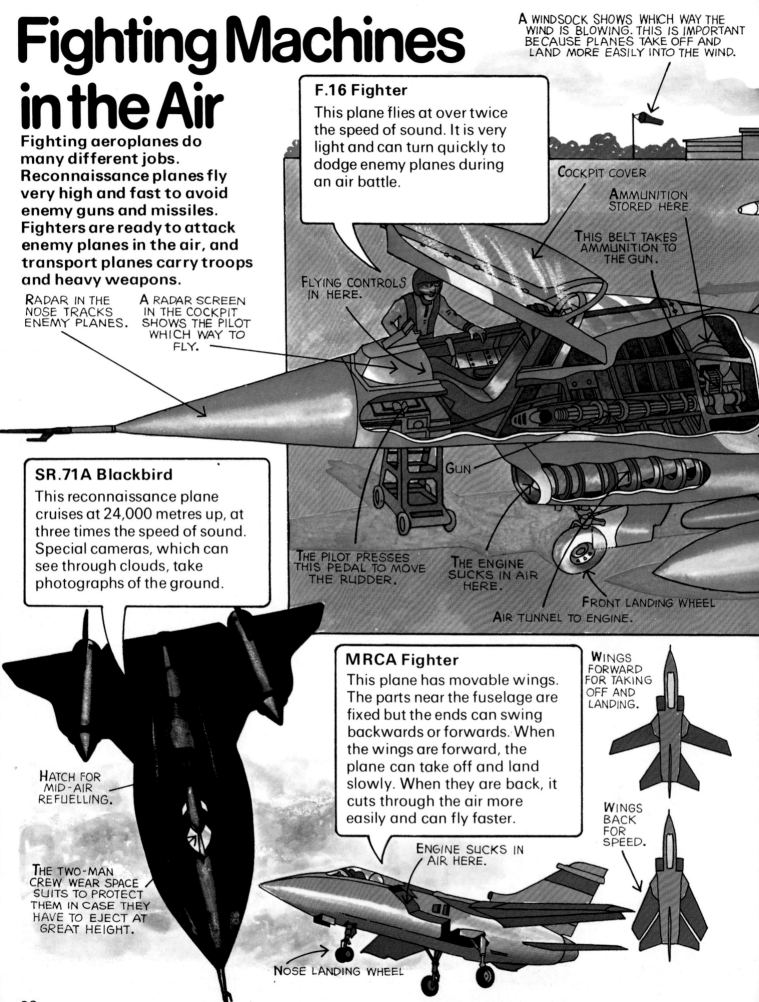

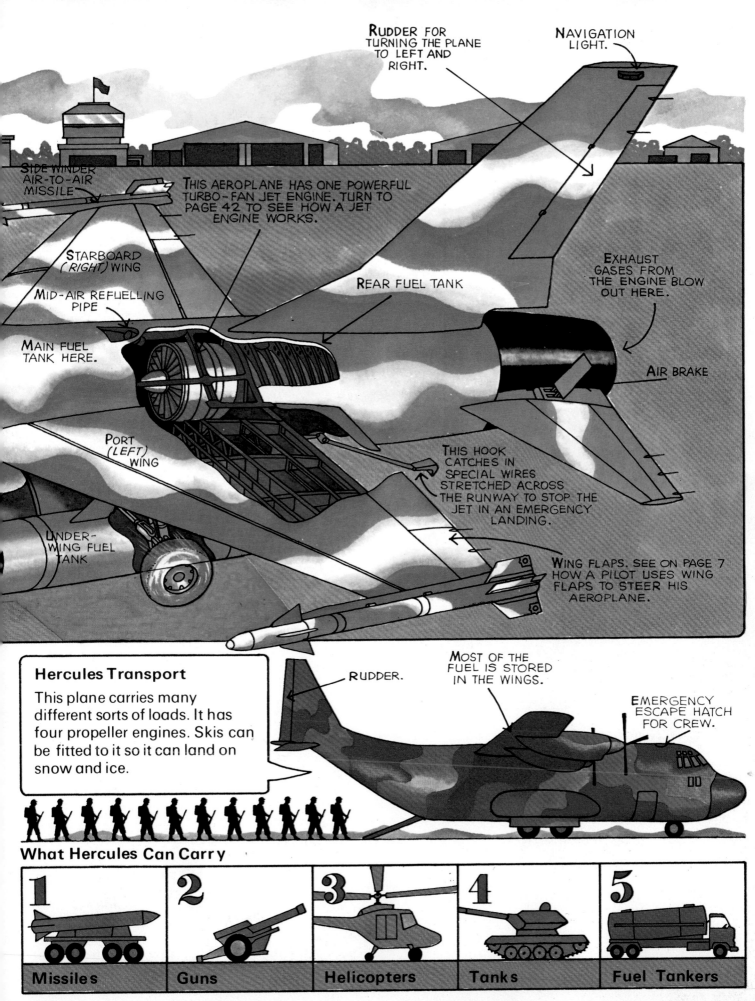

RUDDER FOR TURNING THE PLANE TO LEFT AND RIGHT.

NAVIGATION LIGHT.

SIDE WINDER AIR-TO-AIR MISSILE.

THIS AEROPLANE HAS ONE POWERFUL TURBO-FAN JET ENGINE. TURN TO PAGE 42 TO SEE HOW A JET ENGINE WORKS.

STARBOARD (RIGHT) WING

MID-AIR REFUELLING PIPE

MAIN FUEL TANK HERE.

REAR FUEL TANK

EXHAUST GASES FROM THE ENGINE BLOW OUT HERE.

AIR BRAKE

PORT (LEFT) WING

THIS HOOK CATCHES IN SPECIAL WIRES STRETCHED ACROSS THE RUNWAY TO STOP THE JET IN AN EMERGENCY LANDING.

UNDER-WING FUEL TANK

WING FLAPS. SEE ON PAGE 7 HOW A PILOT USES WING FLAPS TO STEER HIS AEROPLANE.

Hercules Transport

This plane carries many different sorts of loads. It has four propeller engines. Skis can be fitted to it so it can land on snow and ice.

RUDDER.

MOST OF THE FUEL IS STORED IN THE WINGS.

EMERGENCY ESCAPE HATCH FOR CREW.

What Hercules Can Carry

1	2	3	4	5
Missiles	Guns	Helicopters	Tanks	Fuel Tankers

Guided Missile Launcher
Sailors below deck fire the missiles and guide them on to targets by radio signals.

THE HELICOPTER IS COMING INTO LAND ON THE FLIGHT DECK. IT HAS BEEN SEARCHING FOR NEAR-BY ENEMY SHIPS AND SUBMARINES.

THIS AERIAL SENDS OUT AND PICKS UP RADIO MESSAGES. IT CAN INTERCEPT MESSAGES BETWEEN ENEMY SHIPS AND SHORE BASES.

THIS RADAR AERIAL ON THE MAIN MAST BEAMS OUT RADIO WAVES. WHEN THEY HIT A METAL OBJECT, SUCH AS ANOTHER SHIP, THEY BOUNCE BACK TO A RECEIVER. THE OBJECT SHOWS UP ON A SCREEN IN THE OPERATIONS ROOM.

HELICOPTER LANDING DECK

THIS MACHINE TRACKS MISSILES AFTER THEY ARE LAUNCHED. SEAMEN IN THE OPERATING ROOM GUIDE THEM ON TO THEIR TARGET.

THIS SHIP HAS FOUR GAS TURBINE ENGINES—TWO BIG ONES FOR HIGH SPEED AND TWO SMALLER ONES FOR CRUISING.

HELICOPTER HANGAR

RADAR

RUNWAY FOR TAKING OFF AND LANDING.

CONTROL TOWER.

LIFT TO HANGARS BELOW DECK.

SOME AEROPLANES WHICH FLY FROM AIRCRAFT CARRIERS ARE SPECIALLY MADE SO THAT THEY CAN FOLD THEIR WINGS.

Aircraft Carrier
This giant ship is like a floating airport. Jets and helicopters are stored inside and brought up on to deck by lift. Ships like this have a crew of over 2,000 officers, sailors and pilots.

GUIDED MISSILE LAUNCHER.

RADAR

BRIDGE

THE FRONT FLOAT TUCKS IN HERE WHEN THE SHIP IS NOT MOVING.

WATER IS BLOWN OUT HERE.

WATER IS SUCKED IN HERE TO DRIVE THE SHIP ALONG.

FRONT FLOAT

Hydrofoil Ship
This ship has wings, called foils, which are just below the surface. When it is not moving, it sits on the water like an ordinary ship. As it gets up speed it skims along on the foils at up to 90 kph.

Fighting Machines at Sea

Frigate
This fast warship is used to defend slower ships from attack by enemy ships, aircraft and submarines.

The ships sailed by the world's navies have to be ready for action at any time. In a war, they help to defend their country from attack and carry troops and weapons to other countries.

They also protect convoys of cargo ships from enemy ships and submarines. In peace time, the ships have many important jobs, such as mapping the sea bed and rescuing people from accidents at sea.

THE SHIP IS STEERED FROM THE BRIDGE. A MACHINE CALLED AN AUTOPILOT KEEPS IT SAILING IN THE RIGHT DIRECTION, EVEN IN VERY ROUGH WEATHER.

THIS IS THE MAIN GUN. IT FIRES SHELLS UP TO 11 KILOMETRES AWAY. SAILORS BELOW DECK LOAD SHELLS ON TO A CONVEYOR WHICH FEEDS THE GUN. WHEN ELECTRONIC EQUIPMENT HAS WORKED OUT WHERE THE TARGET IS, THE GUN AIMS AND FIRES AUTOMATICALLY.

THE OPERATIONS ROOM IS BELOW THE BRIDGE. DURING A BATTLE THE CAPTAIN CONTROLS THE SHIP FROM HERE.

Nuclear Submarine
This submarine carries enough food and air to go all round the world without coming to the surface. It has a crew of 143. Its 16 missiles can be fired from under the water at targets up to 4,000 kilometres away.

Rescue Machines

These machines have all been specially made to rescue people trapped by fires, in snow, in crashed planes and cars, or from sinking ships. They are always ready for action.

UPPER BOOM

This fire-fighting and rescue machine lifts firemen up to 30 metres above the ground to fight fires and rescue people trapped in tall buildings. It can shoot 2,000 litres of water a minute into a fire.

THIS FIREMAN CAN TURN THE TURNTABLE AND MOVE THE BOOM UP AND DOWN. HE CAN ALSO TALK TO THE FIREMEN IN THE CAGE BY TELEPHONE.

THE PUMP PUSHES WATER UP THIS PIPE WHICH IS FIXED TO THE BOOM.

THE DRIVER RINGS THIS BELL AND BLOWS A SIREN TO WARN OTHER TRAFFIC THAT HE IS ON THE WAY TO A FIRE.

THE PUMP INSIDE THE FIRE ENGINE SUCKS WATER ALONG THIS HOSE.

PUMP

TURNTABLE

THESE LEGS LIFT THE BACK WHEELS OFF THE GROUND AND HOLD THE MACHINE STEADY BEFORE THE BOOM CAN BE RAISED.

THE DIESEL ENGINE IN HERE WORKS THE PUMP. IT ALSO WORKS SPECIAL LIFTING MOTORS WHICH RAISE AND LOWER THE BOOMS.

Motorway Fire Fighter

If there is a bad road crash, a truck like this races to put out the fire. It can shoot out more than 13,000 litres of foam in less than a minute.

Airport Crash Lorry

Firemen use this sort of machine to fight fires in crashed aeroplanes. The machine is full of water and foam. The pump on top shoots foam on to a blazing aeroplane up to 100 metres away. The foam spreads over the flames and smothers them. Small pumps shoot foam round the lorry.

Lifeboat

Specially-trained seamen go out in lifeboats like this to rescue people at sea. Lifeboats are made to stay afloat in even the worst storms. This one has two diesel engines which turn two propellers to drive the boat through the water. See how diesel engines work, on page 45.

Launching a Lifeboat

Some lifeboats are kept in sheds on the seashore. They are launched down a slipway into the sea.

MAST HEAD LIGHT

RADAR SCANNER

THE MAN IN COMMAND IS CALLED THE COXSWAIN. HE STEERS THE BOAT FROM THE WHEELHOUSE.

THE BACK AIRTIGHT COMPARTMENT CARRIES STRETCHERS AND FIRST AID EQUIPMENT FOR INJURED SURVIVORS.

FRONT AIRTIGHT COMPARTMENT IN HERE.

THE HULL OF THIS LIFE BOAT IS MADE OF STEEL. SOME ARE MADE OF WOOD OR GLASSFIBRE.

What Happens if a Lifeboat Capsizes

1 THE TOP PART IS AIRTIGHT. THE HULL IS HEAVY.

A giant wave hits the side of the boat.

2 NOW THE HEAVY HULL IS ON THE SURFACE. THE AIRTIGHT PART IS UNDER WATER.

The boat rolls over. Now it is top heavy.

3 THE HEAVY HULL PUSHES DOWN. THE AIRTIGHT PART PUSHES UP.

It begins to turn the right way up again.

4 THE AIRTIGHT PART IS ABOVE THE WATER AGAIN. THE HEAVY HULL HOLDS THE BOAT DOWN IN THE WATER.

Now the boat is upright again.

Snow Blower

BLADES ON DRUM CUT INTO SNOW.

FAN BLOWS SNOW OUT HERE.

This machine makes paths through snow up to 1.3 metres deep. The drum turns round very fast and cuts through the snow. A fan blows it out sideways.

Mountain Rescue Aeroplane

Small aeroplanes with skis can land on the snow on high mountains. They rescue injured climbers and people trapped by storms and avalanches.

Building Machines

Tall buildings need strong foundations deep in the ground for them to stand on. The crane and drilling machine on this building site are boring holes for the concrete foundations.

JIB

FRAME

DRILL

One end of this wire rope is fixed to the drum inside the crane. The other end is fixed to the top of the drill bar. As the crane motor turns the drum, the wire rope raises or lowers the drill bar.

JIB

THESE WIRES FROM THE FRAME HOLD UP THE END OF THE JIB.

DRUM

DIESEL ENGINE IN HERE

TURNTABLE

This man is checking that the drill bar is working properly. The holes for the foundations have to be drilled in exactly the right places. These are drawn on the plans of the building and then worked out on the ground.

The crane driver controls the diesel engine which does three different jobs. It turns the crawler tracks which move the crane along. It turns the drum to raise and lower the drill bar, and it swings the crane round on its turntable.

THE CRANE STANDS FIRM ON CRAWLER TRACKS. THEY STOP IT SINKING INTO THE GROUND.

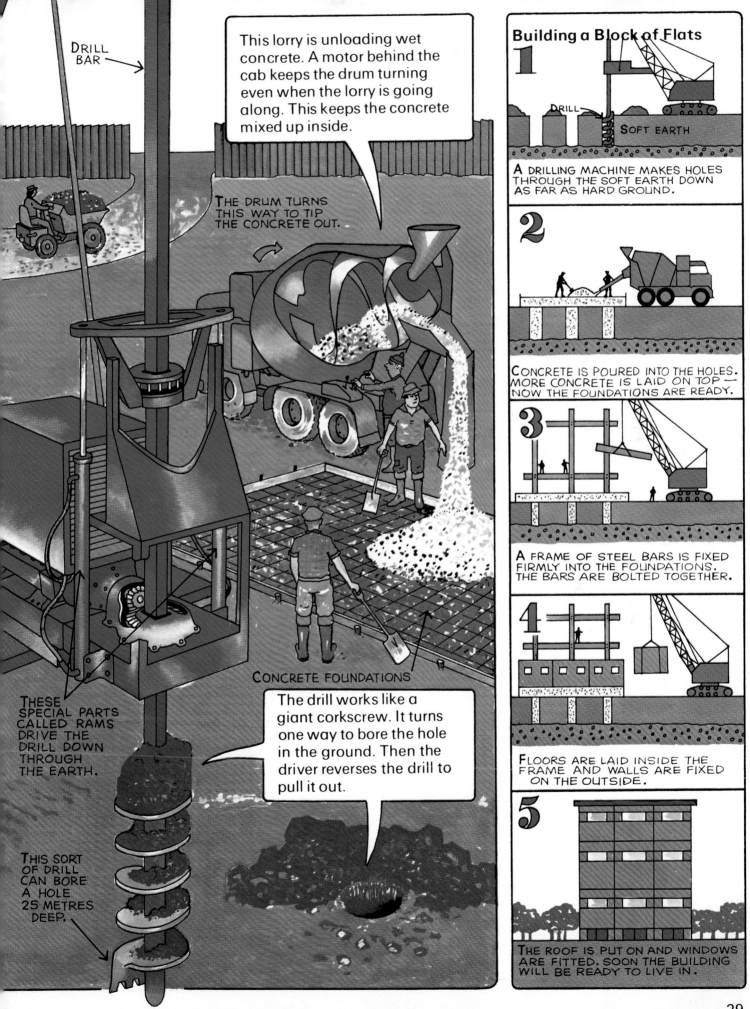

DRILL BAR

This lorry is unloading wet concrete. A motor behind the cab keeps the drum turning even when the lorry is going along. This keeps the concrete mixed up inside.

THE DRUM TURNS THIS WAY TO TIP THE CONCRETE OUT.

THESE SPECIAL PARTS CALLED RAMS DRIVE THE DRILL DOWN THROUGH THE EARTH.

CONCRETE FOUNDATIONS

The drill works like a giant corkscrew. It turns one way to bore the hole in the ground. Then the driver reverses the drill to pull it out.

THIS SORT OF DRILL CAN BORE A HOLE 25 METRES DEEP.

Building a Block of Flats

1 DRILL — SOFT EARTH

A DRILLING MACHINE MAKES HOLES THROUGH THE SOFT EARTH DOWN AS FAR AS HARD GROUND.

2

CONCRETE IS POURED INTO THE HOLES. MORE CONCRETE IS LAID ON TOP — NOW THE FOUNDATIONS ARE READY.

3

A FRAME OF STEEL BARS IS FIXED FIRMLY INTO THE FOUNDATIONS. THE BARS ARE BOLTED TOGETHER.

4

FLOORS ARE LAID INSIDE THE FRAME AND WALLS ARE FIXED ON THE OUTSIDE.

5

THE ROOF IS PUT ON AND WINDOWS ARE FITTED. SOON THE BUILDING WILL BE READY TO LIVE IN.

29

Road Making

Motorways are specially built so that cars and very heavy lorries can speed safely along them. They have to be level with strong foundations.

Follow the numbers at the bottom of the page. They show how the different machines are used to carve out a new road. First they prepare the ground. Then they build up a motorway on the top.

The blade underneath this grader smooths out the ground. It is slightly tilted so the road will slope from the middle to the sides.

This asphalt machine is pushing the lorry slowly in front of it. As the hot asphalt tips out, the machine spreads it on while it is soft.

ARMS

DIESEL ENGINE

HOOKS LIKE THIS AT THE BACK ARE USED TO DRAG OUT TREE ROOTS OR BIG BOULDERS.

The bulldozer driver uses the big blade at the front to push earth and rocks out of the way. The blade is worked by long arms which move it up and down and tip it forwards and backwards.

Bulldozers have crawler tracks like tanks. The tracks are made of steel and fit over the wheels. They stop bulldozers sinking and help them to push heavy loads when the ground is very soft or muddy.

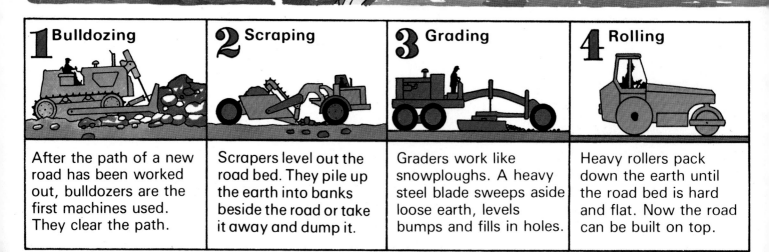

1 Bulldozing

After the path of a new road has been worked out, bulldozers are the first machines used. They clear the path.

2 Scraping

Scrapers level out the road bed. They pile up the earth into banks beside the road or take it away and dump it.

3 Grading

Graders work like snowploughs. A heavy steel blade sweeps aside loose earth, levels bumps and fills in holes.

4 Rolling

Heavy rollers pack down the earth until the road bed is hard and flat. Now the road can be built on top.

This giant scraper levels out the ground. It scoops up huge loads of earth, takes them away and dumps them. A diesel engine drives the scraper along, turns the paddles round and raises and lowers the blade. See how a diesel engine works on page 45.

EARTH IS PILED UP BESIDE THE TRENCH. IT WILL BE PUT BACK AFTER THE DRAINS HAVE BEEN PUT IN.

An excavator is digging a trench for drains. Roads slope down from the middle so rain water will run off at each side.

THE PADDLES WORK LIKE A MOVING STAIRCASE. THEY PICK UP THE EARTH AND DROP IT INTO THE BOWL.

BOWL

PADDLES

BLADE

DIESEL ENGINE

The blade is fixed across the front of the bowl. When the driver lowers the bowl, the blade slices off the top layer of earth as the scraper goes along.

Deep grooves in the tyres help the scraper to grip when it is carrying a heavy load.

5 Laying Stones

Tipper lorries bring loads of crushed stones. Then a machine called a flicker is driven slowly over the stones. It flicks the stones forward and spreads them out evenly.

6 Rolling

Next the stones are rolled again so that the base of the road is firm. Now it is ready for the top surface to be laid.

7 Laying Asphalt

Asphalt is a tough sticky mixture which sets very hard when it gets cold. Some motorways are made of concrete instead of stones and asphalt.

Mining and Excavating

Lots of valuable metals and minerals, such as gold, copper, coal and diamonds, lie buried in the ground. Some are only a few metres down. Giant shovels and excavators dig them out at open surface mines.

Some things are found thousands of metres under the ground. Miners dig deep shafts down to reach them. Underground mining is dangerous because tunnels can cave in and gases in mines cause explosions.

Bucket Wheel Excavator

This giant machine digs on the surface. It has 26 electric motors to make all the parts work. It uses as much electricity as a small town and needs 13 men to work it. See how electric motors work on page 45.

Tunneller

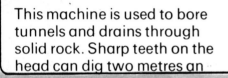

DIGGING HEAD

ELECTRIC MOTOR

THIS TUBE SUCKS OUT DUST

DRIVER

This machine is used to bore tunnels and drains through solid rock. Sharp teeth on the head can dig two metres an hour. Pieces of rock are pushed out of the tunnel on a conveyor under the machine.

THESE WIRE ROPES RAISE AND LOWER THE DIGGING ARM.

THE LOAD FALLS OUT OF EACH BUCKET WHEN IT REACHES THE TOP OF THE WHEEL.

EACH BUCKET LOAD SLIDES DOWN A SHUTE ON TO THE BEGINNING OF THE CONVEYOR.

TWO MEN IN THIS CABIN CONTROL THE BUCKET WHEEL.

THE BUCKET WHEEL IS 20 METRES HIGH. IT HAS 18 BUCKETS. WHEN THE WHEEL GOES ROUND, THE BUCKETS DIG INTO THE GROUND.

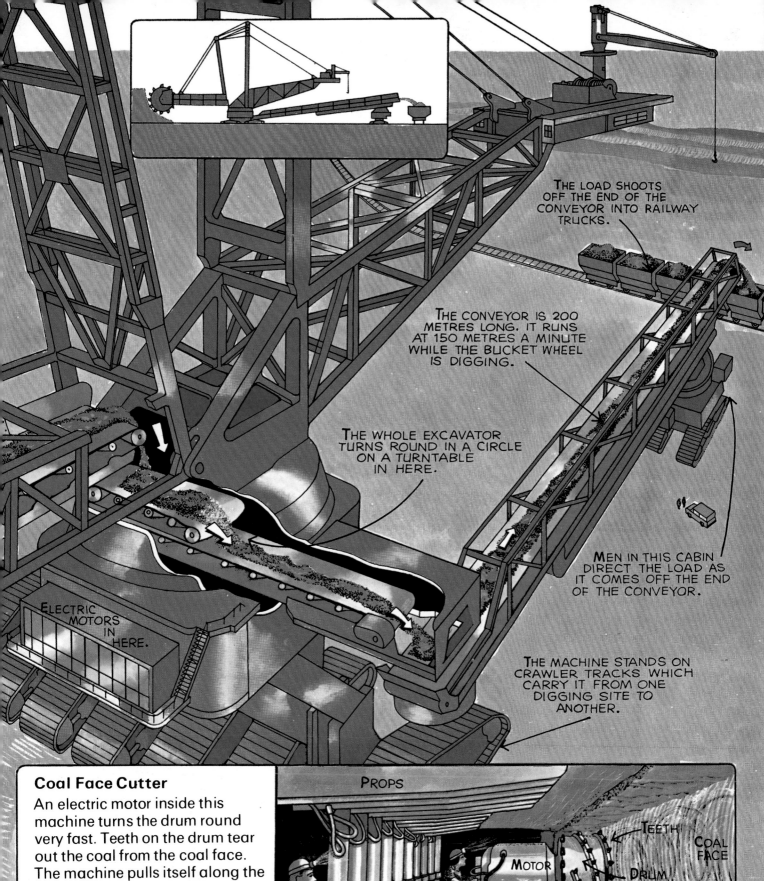

THE LOAD SHOOTS OFF THE END OF THE CONVEYOR INTO RAILWAY TRUCKS.

THE CONVEYOR IS 200 METRES LONG. IT RUNS AT 150 METRES A MINUTE WHILE THE BUCKET WHEEL IS DIGGING.

THE WHOLE EXCAVATOR TURNS ROUND IN A CIRCLE ON A TURNTABLE IN HERE.

ELECTRIC MOTORS IN HERE.

MEN IN THIS CABIN DIRECT THE LOAD AS IT COMES OFF THE END OF THE CONVEYOR.

THE MACHINE STANDS ON CRAWLER TRACKS WHICH CARRY IT FROM ONE DIGGING SITE TO ANOTHER.

Coal Face Cutter

An electric motor inside this machine turns the drum round very fast. Teeth on the drum tear out the coal from the coal face. The machine pulls itself along the chain beside the rails. Miners work the levers which push the props forward and hold up the roof after the machine goes past.

PROPS

TEETH

COAL FACE

MOTOR

DRUM

CHAIN

33

Oil from Under the Sea

The men on this oil rig are drilling a hole to find oil under the sea. A test of the rock below the sea bed has shown them where to look for oil.

Two sorts of rig are needed to get oil ashore. When a drilling rig has found oil, tugs come and tow it away. Then a production rig is used to pump the oil out of the ground.

The derrick holds the top of the drilling pipe steady as the motor drives it into the ground.

This crane is lifting a new piece of drilling pipe into the derrick.

HELICOPTER DECK

This is the engine room. Special machines make electricity for the whole rig and drive the drill.

This pipe carries mud from the tank to the drill pipe.

PUMPS

CONTROL ROOM

This is the drilling pipe. It goes all the way down through the sea bed. As the drill goes deeper, rigmen add more pieces of pipe.

MUD PUMPS

These giant feet are now underwater. Pumps at the top of the legs have filled them with sea water. The weight of the water in the feet keeps the rig steady even when the weather is stormy.

ANCHOR

WELL-HEAD

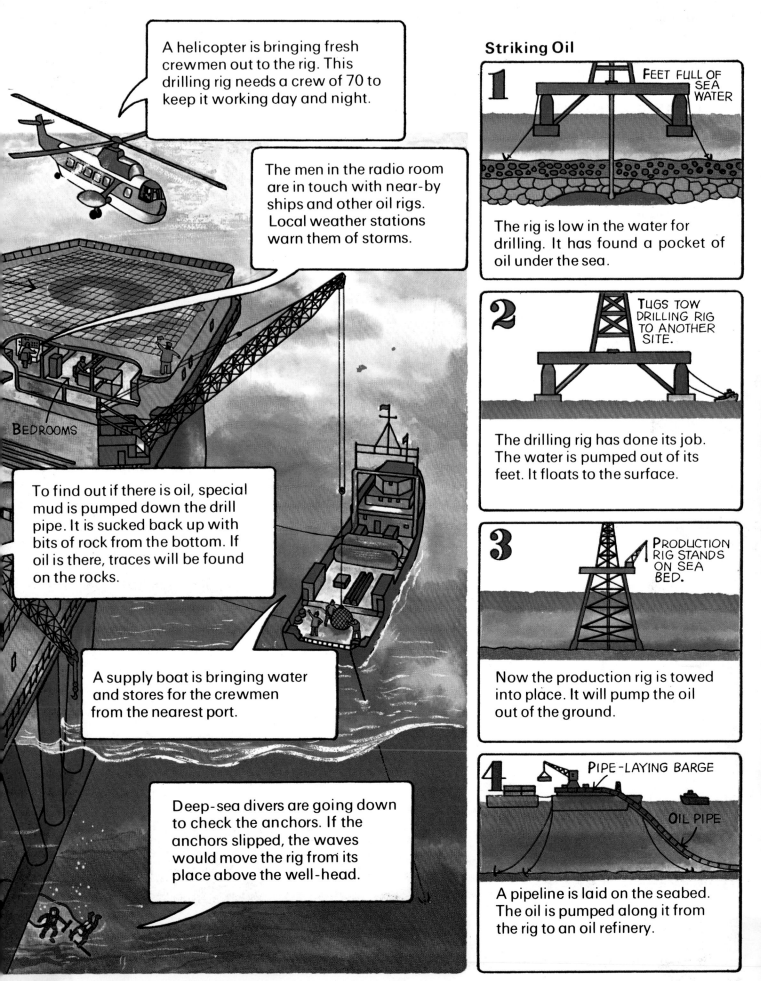

A helicopter is bringing fresh crewmen out to the rig. This drilling rig needs a crew of 70 to keep it working day and night.

The men in the radio room are in touch with near-by ships and other oil rigs. Local weather stations warn them of storms.

BEDROOMS

To find out if there is oil, special mud is pumped down the drill pipe. It is sucked back up with bits of rock from the bottom. If oil is there, traces will be found on the rocks.

A supply boat is bringing water and stores for the crewmen from the nearest port.

Deep-sea divers are going down to check the anchors. If the anchors slipped, the waves would move the rig from its place above the well-head.

Striking Oil

1 FEET FULL OF SEA WATER

The rig is low in the water for drilling. It has found a pocket of oil under the sea.

2 TUGS TOW DRILLING RIG TO ANOTHER SITE.

The drilling rig has done its job. The water is pumped out of its feet. It floats to the surface.

3 PRODUCTION RIG STANDS ON SEA BED.

Now the production rig is towed into place. It will pump the oil out of the ground.

4 PIPE-LAYING BARGE

OIL PIPE

A pipeline is laid on the seabed. The oil is pumped along it from the rig to an oil refinery.

Farming Machines

Farmers use lots of machines to prepare their land, sow seeds and harvest the crops.

Follow the numbers at the bottom of the page to see how a farmer grows a crop of wheat.

Tractors and combine harvesters have diesel engines. See how they work on page 45.

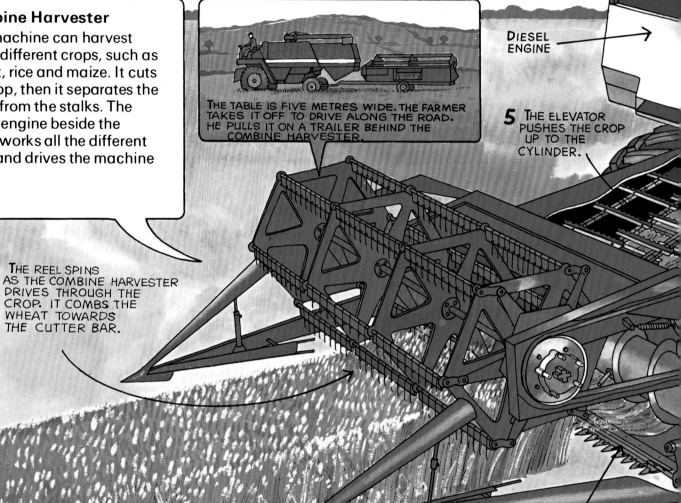

Combine Harvester

This machine can harvest many different crops, such as wheat, rice and maize. It cuts the crop, then it separates the seeds from the stalks. The diesel engine beside the driver works all the different parts and drives the machine along.

THE TABLE IS FIVE METRES WIDE. THE FARMER TAKES IT OFF TO DRIVE ALONG THE ROAD. HE PULLS IT ON A TRAILER BEHIND THE COMBINE HARVESTER.

DIESEL ENGINE

5 THE ELEVATOR PUSHES THE CROP UP TO THE CYLINDER.

1 THE REEL SPINS AS THE COMBINE HARVESTER DRIVES THROUGH THE CROP. IT COMBS THE WHEAT TOWARDS THE CUTTER BAR.

2 THE KNIFE IN THE CUTTER BAR MOVES FROM SIDE TO SIDE VERY QUICKLY TO CUT THE STALKS.

1 Ploughing

In winter and spring, farmers use ploughs to break up the soil. Blades cut into the ground and turn it over in furrows.

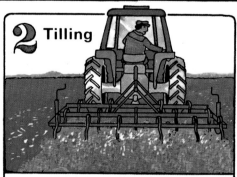

2 Tilling

Clods of earth left by the plough are broken up into small pieces. Now the soil is level and ready for the seeds.

3 Sowing

This long box is full of seeds and fertilizer. As the tractor pulls the drill along, each tube sows a row of seeds.

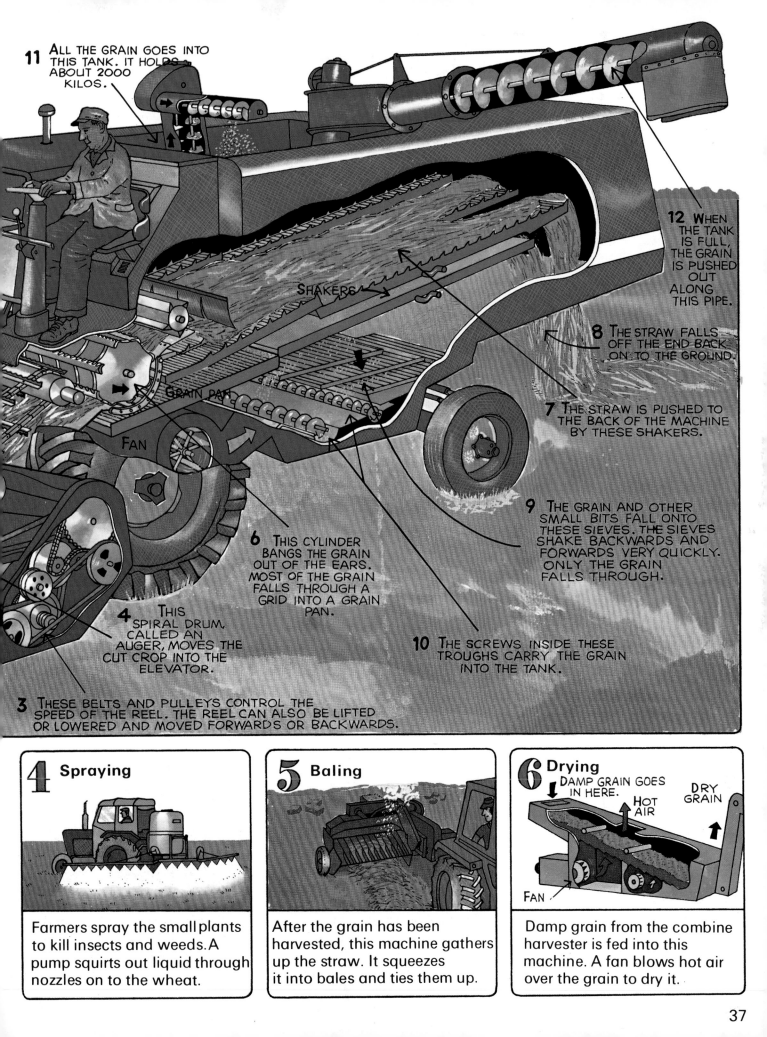

11 ALL THE GRAIN GOES INTO THIS TANK. IT HOLDS ABOUT 2000 KILOS.

12 WHEN THE TANK IS FULL, THE GRAIN IS PUSHED OUT ALONG THIS PIPE.

SHAKERS

8 THE STRAW FALLS OFF THE END BACK ON TO THE GROUND.

7 THE STRAW IS PUSHED TO THE BACK OF THE MACHINE BY THESE SHAKERS.

GRAIN PAN

FAN

9 THE GRAIN AND OTHER SMALL BITS FALL ONTO THESE SIEVES. THE SIEVES SHAKE BACKWARDS AND FORWARDS VERY QUICKLY. ONLY THE GRAIN FALLS THROUGH.

6 THIS CYLINDER BANGS THE GRAIN OUT OF THE EARS. MOST OF THE GRAIN FALLS THROUGH A GRID INTO A GRAIN PAN.

4 THIS SPIRAL DRUM, CALLED AN AUGER, MOVES THE CUT CROP INTO THE ELEVATOR.

10 THE SCREWS INSIDE THESE TROUGHS CARRY THE GRAIN INTO THE TANK.

3 THESE BELTS AND PULLEYS CONTROL THE SPEED OF THE REEL. THE REEL CAN ALSO BE LIFTED OR LOWERED AND MOVED FORWARDS OR BACKWARDS.

4 Spraying

Farmers spray the small plants to kill insects and weeds. A pump squirts out liquid through nozzles on to the wheat.

5 Baling

After the grain has been harvested, this machine gathers up the straw. It squeezes it into bales and ties them up.

6 Drying

DAMP GRAIN GOES IN HERE.

HOT AIR

DRY GRAIN

FAN

Damp grain from the combine harvester is fed into this machine. A fan blows hot air over the grain to dry it.

37

Dairy Machines

This modern milking machine helps farmers to milk their cows quickly and easily. An electric motor turns the whole machine slowly round with the cows standing on it. Follow the numbers to see how all the different parts work. Turn to page 45 to see how an electric motor works.

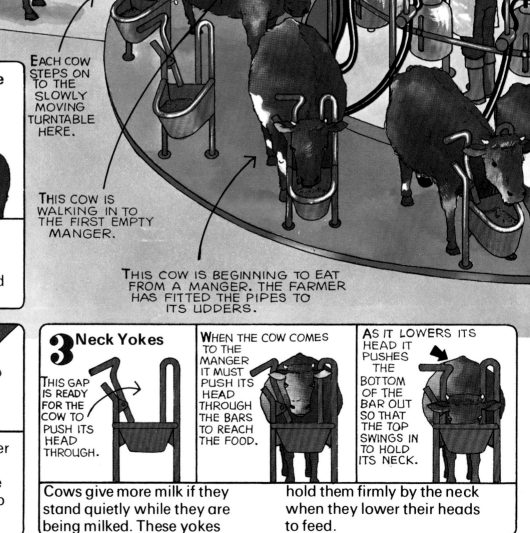

WHEN THE COWS HAVE NO MORE MILK TO GIVE, THE FARMER TAKES OFF THE PIPES.

COWS GO OUT THIS WAY

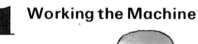

COWS STEP OFF THE MACHINE HERE.

COWS COME IN HERE.

A SPECIAL GATE LETS THEM IN ONE AT A TIME

EACH COW STEPS ON TO THE SLOWLY MOVING TURNTABLE HERE.

THIS COW IS WALKING IN TO THE FIRST EMPTY MANGER.

THIS COW IS BEGINNING TO EAT FROM A MANGER. THE FARMER HAS FITTED THE PIPES TO ITS UDDERS.

1 Working the Machine

CONTROL PANELS

The farmer stands in the middle of the machine. He makes it start and stop. He dials the right amount of food for each cow.

2 Feeding

PELLETS OF SPECIAL FOOD FALL DOWN A SHUTE FROM THE LOFT INTO EACH MANGER.

Cows eat grass in the summer and hay in the winter. Farmers also give them some special food each day to help them make extra milk.

3 Neck Yokes

THIS GAP IS READY FOR THE COW TO PUSH ITS HEAD THROUGH.

WHEN THE COW COMES TO THE MANGER IT MUST PUSH ITS HEAD THROUGH THE BARS TO REACH THE FOOD.

AS IT LOWERS ITS HEAD IT PUSHES THE BOTTOM OF THE BAR OUT SO THAT THE TOP SWINGS IN TO HOLD ITS NECK.

Cows give more milk if they stand quietly while they are being milked. These yokes hold them firmly by the neck when they lower their heads to feed.

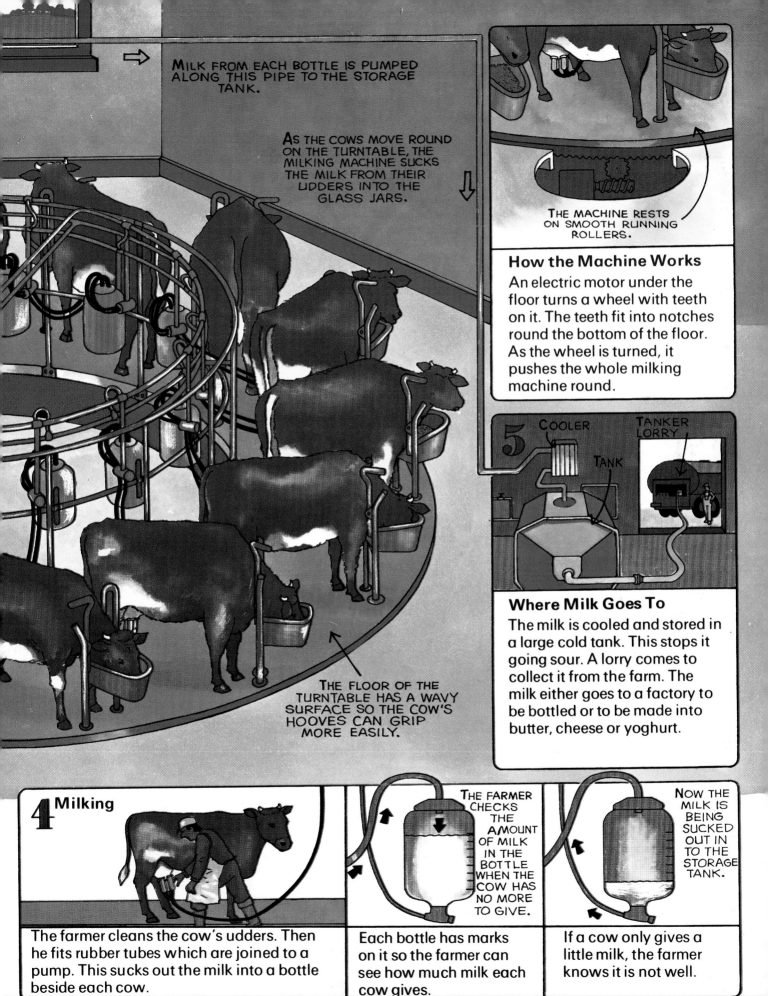

MILK FROM EACH BOTTLE IS PUMPED ALONG THIS PIPE TO THE STORAGE TANK.

AS THE COWS MOVE ROUND ON THE TURNTABLE, THE MILKING MACHINE SUCKS THE MILK FROM THEIR UDDERS INTO THE GLASS JARS.

THE MACHINE RESTS ON SMOOTH RUNNING ROLLERS.

How the Machine Works

An electric motor under the floor turns a wheel with teeth on it. The teeth fit into notches round the bottom of the floor. As the wheel is turned, it pushes the whole milking machine round.

THE FLOOR OF THE TURNTABLE HAS A WAVY SURFACE SO THE COW'S HOOVES CAN GRIP MORE EASILY.

5 COOLER TANKER LORRY TANK

Where Milk Goes To

The milk is cooled and stored in a large cold tank. This stops it going sour. A lorry comes to collect it from the farm. The milk either goes to a factory to be bottled or to be made into butter, cheese or yoghurt.

4 Milking

The farmer cleans the cow's udders. Then he fits rubber tubes which are joined to a pump. This sucks out the milk into a bottle beside each cow.

THE FARMER CHECKS THE AMOUNT OF MILK IN THE BOTTLE WHEN THE COW HAS NO MORE TO GIVE.

Each bottle has marks on it so the farmer can see how much milk each cow gives.

NOW THE MILK IS BEING SUCKED OUT IN TO THE STORAGE TANK.

If a cow only gives a little milk, the farmer knows it is not well.

Home Machines

Television

1 Television pictures are taken by a television camera. The music, singing and talking are recorded at the same time. These sounds and the pictures are then turned into electric signals.

2 A television mast beams out the signals through the air. Every set has an aerial which picks up the signals.

TELEVISION MAST

AERIAL

A television set works by electricity. When the set is switched on, it changes the signals back into pictures and sounds again. The sounds come out of the loudspeaker and the pictures appear on the screen.

THE SCREEN IS THE FRONT OF THE GLASS TUBE. IT IS COATED WITH THOUSANDS OF TINY DOTS. WHEN THE SIGNALS HIT THE DOTS, THEY TURN BACK INTO PICTURES AGAIN.

THIS ELECTRIC GUN SHOOTS THE PICTURE SIGNALS DOWN THE GLASS TUBE.

FLAT PIECES OF METAL STEER THE SIGNALS ON TO THE SCREEN.

THE SIGNALS COME IN HERE FROM THE AERIAL.

ELECTRICITY COMES IN HERE TO MAKE THE TELEVISION WORK.

LOUDSPEAKER

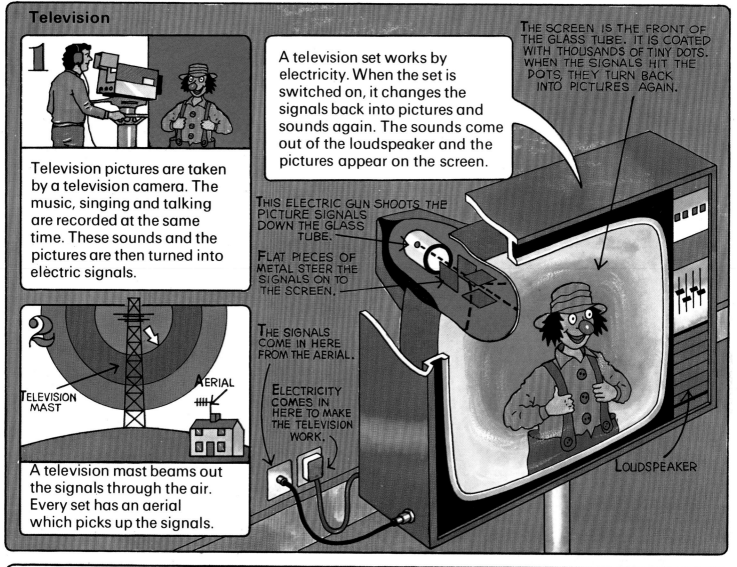

Telephone

When you speak, the words make sound waves in the air. When you speak into a telephone, special parts in the mouthpiece turn the waves into electric signals. With the help of electricity, these signals travel down telephone wires. Special parts in the earpiece at the other end turn the signals back into speech.

EARPIECE

PLATE

THESE BUTTONS SWITCH THE TELEPHONE ON AND OFF.

ELECTRICITY IN HERE TURNS THE SOUND WAVES INTO ELECTRIC SIGNALS WHICH GO DOWN THE WIRE.

ELECTRIC SIGNALS COME DOWN THESE WIRES TO THE EARPIECE. THEY MAKE THE PLATE MOVE UP AND DOWN. THIS TURNS THE SIGNALS BACK INTO WORDS.

ELECTRICITY COMES IN HERE.

THE WORDS YOU SPEAK MAKE THIS FLAT PIECE OF METAL FLAP UP AND DOWN.

MOUTHPIECE

Refrigerator

A refrigerator is very cold inside because all the warmth is taken out of the air in it. This is done by a special liquid which is pumped through a pipe at the back. Follow the numbers to see how the liquid changes as it goes round inside the pipe.

1 THE LIQUID CHANGES INTO GAS HERE AND EVAPORATES. AS IT CHANGES IT TAKES THE HEAT OUT OF THE AIR IN THE REFRIGERATOR.

2 THIS MACHINE, CALLED A COMPRESSOR, SUCKS THE GAS DOWN THE PIPE. IT SQUEEZES IT AND PUSHES IT INTO THE CONDENSER.

3 THIS SMALL ELECTRIC MOTOR DRIVES THE COMPRESSOR. SEE HOW AN ELECTRIC MOTOR WORKS ON PAGE 45.

4 NOW THE GAS TURNS BACK INTO LIQUID INSIDE THE CONDENSER.

5 NOW THE LIQUID IS READY TO GO ROUND THE PIPE AGAIN.

THE WALLS AND DOOR OF A REFRIGERATOR ARE SPECIALLY THICK TO KEEP THE COLD IN.

Lavatory

The water tank above a lavatory is called a cistern. This one is full of water because the handle is up.

Now the handle is down. It has pulled up the plunger and forced the water through the pipe to the bowl.

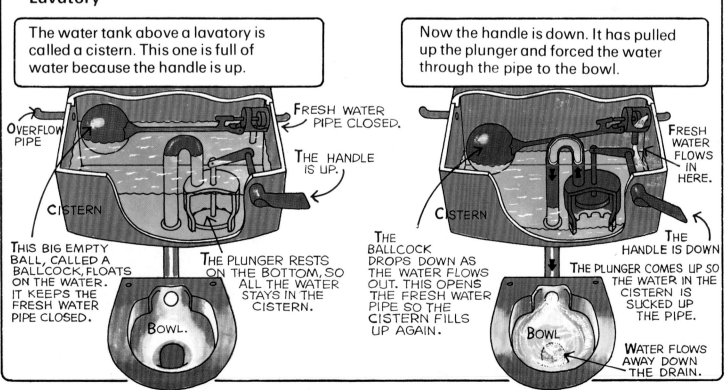

OVERFLOW PIPE

FRESH WATER PIPE CLOSED.

THE HANDLE IS UP.

CISTERN

THIS BIG EMPTY BALL, CALLED A BALLCOCK, FLOATS ON THE WATER. IT KEEPS THE FRESH WATER PIPE CLOSED.

THE PLUNGER RESTS ON THE BOTTOM, SO ALL THE WATER STAYS IN THE CISTERN.

BOWL.

FRESH WATER FLOWS IN HERE.

CISTERN

THE BALLCOCK DROPS DOWN AS THE WATER FLOWS OUT. THIS OPENS THE FRESH WATER PIPE SO THE CISTERN FILLS UP AGAIN.

THE HANDLE IS DOWN

THE PLUNGER COMES UP SO THE WATER IN THE CISTERN IS SUCKED UP THE PIPE.

BOWL

WATER FLOWS AWAY DOWN THE DRAIN.

How Motors Work

Jet Engines

Most jet aircraft have gas turbine engines. They burn special fuel called kerosene in a combustion chamber. As the kerosene burns, it makes hot gases which are blown out of the back of the engine. They push the plane through the air.

Follow the numbers in the pictures to see how three different jet engines work.

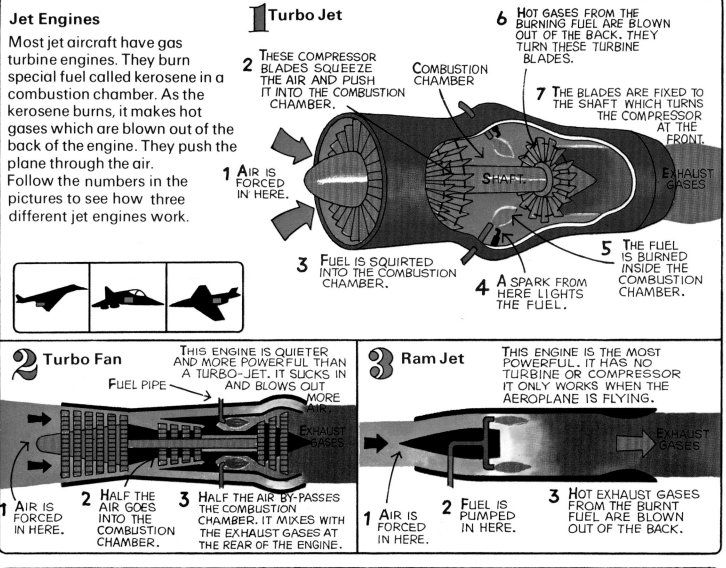

1 Turbo Jet

2 THESE COMPRESSOR BLADES SQUEEZE THE AIR AND PUSH IT INTO THE COMBUSTION CHAMBER.

COMBUSTION CHAMBER

6 HOT GASES FROM THE BURNING FUEL ARE BLOWN OUT OF THE BACK. THEY TURN THESE TURBINE BLADES.

7 THE BLADES ARE FIXED TO THE SHAFT WHICH TURNS THE COMPRESSOR AT THE FRONT.

1 AIR IS FORCED IN HERE.

SHAFT.

EXHAUST GASES

3 FUEL IS SQUIRTED INTO THE COMBUSTION CHAMBER.

4 A SPARK FROM HERE LIGHTS THE FUEL.

5 THE FUEL IS BURNED INSIDE THE COMBUSTION CHAMBER.

2 Turbo Fan

THIS ENGINE IS QUIETER AND MORE POWERFUL THAN A TURBO-JET. IT SUCKS IN AND BLOWS OUT MORE AIR.

FUEL PIPE

EXHAUST GASES

1 AIR IS FORCED IN HERE.

2 HALF THE AIR GOES INTO THE COMBUSTION CHAMBER.

3 HALF THE AIR BY-PASSES THE COMBUSTION CHAMBER. IT MIXES WITH THE EXHAUST GASES AT THE REAR OF THE ENGINE.

3 Ram Jet

THIS ENGINE IS THE MOST POWERFUL. IT HAS NO TURBINE OR COMPRESSOR IT ONLY WORKS WHEN THE AEROPLANE IS FLYING.

EXHAUST GASES

1 AIR IS FORCED IN HERE.

2 FUEL IS PUMPED IN HERE.

3 HOT EXHAUST GASES FROM THE BURNT FUEL ARE BLOWN OUT OF THE BACK.

Steam Turbine

These sorts of engines are used to turn ships' propellers and to make electricity in power stations. Rings of turbine blades are fixed to a shaft inside a steam-tight cylinder. Steam from a boiler is blasted against the blades which spin the shaft round very fast. As the steam passes through the cylinder it gets cooler and expands. So each ring of turbine blades is slightly bigger than the one before.

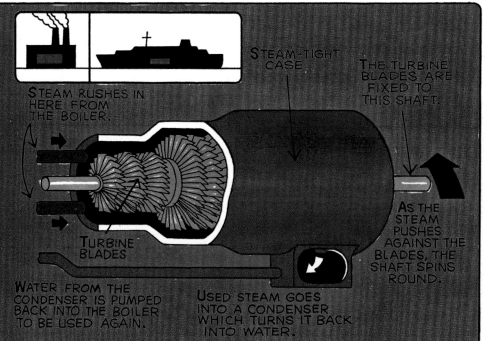

STEAM RUSHES IN HERE FROM THE BOILER.

STEAM-TIGHT CASE

THE TURBINE BLADES ARE FIXED TO THIS SHAFT.

TURBINE BLADES

AS THE STEAM PUSHES AGAINST THE BLADES, THE SHAFT SPINS ROUND.

WATER FROM THE CONDENSER IS PUMPED BACK INTO THE BOILER TO BE USED AGAIN.

USED STEAM GOES INTO A CONDENSER WHICH TURNS IT BACK INTO WATER.

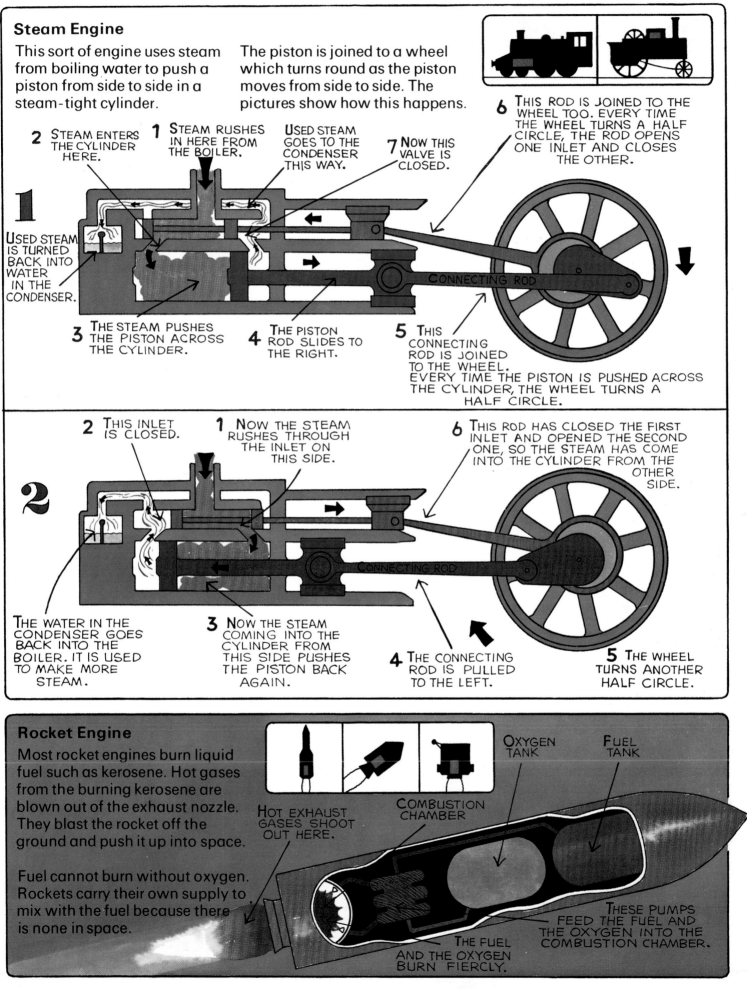

Steam Engine

This sort of engine uses steam from boiling water to push a piston from side to side in a steam-tight cylinder.

The piston is joined to a wheel which turns round as the piston moves from side to side. The pictures show how this happens.

1

2 STEAM ENTERS THE CYLINDER HERE.

1 STEAM RUSHES IN HERE FROM THE BOILER.

USED STEAM GOES TO THE CONDENSER THIS WAY.

7 NOW THIS VALVE IS CLOSED.

6 THIS ROD IS JOINED TO THE WHEEL TOO. EVERY TIME THE WHEEL TURNS A HALF CIRCLE, THE ROD OPENS ONE INLET AND CLOSES THE OTHER.

USED STEAM IS TURNED BACK INTO WATER IN THE CONDENSER.

3 THE STEAM PUSHES THE PISTON ACROSS THE CYLINDER.

4 THE PISTON ROD SLIDES TO THE RIGHT.

CONNECTING ROD

5 THIS CONNECTING ROD IS JOINED TO THE WHEEL. EVERY TIME THE PISTON IS PUSHED ACROSS THE CYLINDER, THE WHEEL TURNS A HALF CIRCLE.

2

2 THIS INLET IS CLOSED.

1 NOW THE STEAM RUSHES THROUGH THE INLET ON THIS SIDE.

6 THIS ROD HAS CLOSED THE FIRST INLET AND OPENED THE SECOND ONE, SO THE STEAM HAS COME INTO THE CYLINDER FROM THE OTHER SIDE.

THE WATER IN THE CONDENSER GOES BACK INTO THE BOILER. IT IS USED TO MAKE MORE STEAM.

3 NOW THE STEAM COMING INTO THE CYLINDER FROM THIS SIDE PUSHES THE PISTON BACK AGAIN.

CONNECTING ROD

4 THE CONNECTING ROD IS PULLED TO THE LEFT.

5 THE WHEEL TURNS ANOTHER HALF CIRCLE.

Rocket Engine

Most rocket engines burn liquid fuel such as kerosene. Hot gases from the burning kerosene are blown out of the exhaust nozzle. They blast the rocket off the ground and push it up into space.

Fuel cannot burn without oxygen. Rockets carry their own supply to mix with the fuel because there is none in space.

HOT EXHAUST GASES SHOOT OUT HERE.

COMBUSTION CHAMBER

OXYGEN TANK

FUEL TANK

THESE PUMPS FEED THE FUEL AND THE OXYGEN INTO THE COMBUSTION CHAMBER.

THE FUEL AND THE OXYGEN BURN FIERCLY.

How Motors Work

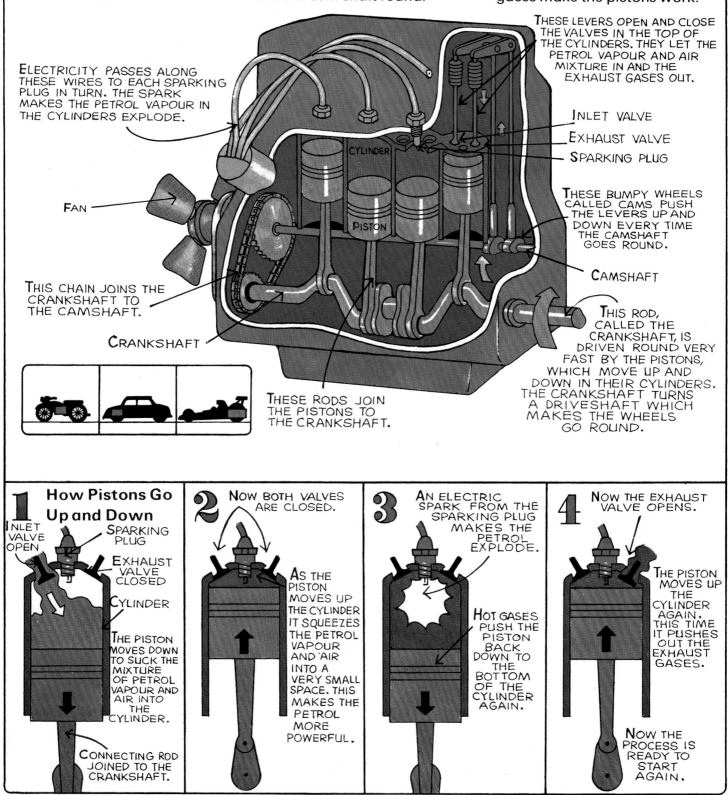

Petrol Engine

This sort of engine turns the wheels of most cars round. It has four cylinders. Each one has a piston inside which is joined to the cam shaft.

The pistons are pushed up and down very quickly inside the cylinders. As they move up and down one after the other, they turn the cam shaft round.

Follow the numbers at the bottom of the page to see what happens when the petrol vapour explodes. See how the exhaust gases make the pistons work.

ELECTRICITY PASSES ALONG THESE WIRES TO EACH SPARKING PLUG IN TURN. THE SPARK MAKES THE PETROL VAPOUR IN THE CYLINDERS EXPLODE.

FAN

THIS CHAIN JOINS THE CRANKSHAFT TO THE CAMSHAFT.

CRANKSHAFT

THESE RODS JOIN THE PISTONS TO THE CRANKSHAFT.

CYLINDER

PISTON

THESE LEVERS OPEN AND CLOSE THE VALVES IN THE TOP OF THE CYLINDERS. THEY LET THE PETROL VAPOUR AND AIR MIXTURE IN AND THE EXHAUST GASES OUT.

INLET VALVE
EXHAUST VALVE
SPARKING PLUG

THESE BUMPY WHEELS CALLED CAMS PUSH THE LEVERS UP AND DOWN EVERY TIME THE CAMSHAFT GOES ROUND.

CAMSHAFT

THIS ROD, CALLED THE CRANKSHAFT, IS DRIVEN ROUND VERY FAST BY THE PISTONS, WHICH MOVE UP AND DOWN IN THEIR CYLINDERS. THE CRANKSHAFT TURNS A DRIVESHAFT WHICH MAKES THE WHEELS GO ROUND.

1 How Pistons Go Up and Down

INLET VALVE OPEN
SPARKING PLUG
EXHAUST VALVE CLOSED
CYLINDER

THE PISTON MOVES DOWN TO SUCK THE MIXTURE OF PETROL VAPOUR AND AIR INTO THE CYLINDER.

CONNECTING ROD JOINED TO THE CRANKSHAFT.

2 NOW BOTH VALVES ARE CLOSED.

AS THE PISTON MOVES UP THE CYLINDER IT SQUEEZES THE PETROL VAPOUR AND AIR INTO A VERY SMALL SPACE. THIS MAKES THE PETROL MORE POWERFUL.

3 AN ELECTRIC SPARK FROM THE SPARKING PLUG MAKES THE PETROL EXPLODE.

HOT GASES PUSH THE PISTON BACK DOWN TO THE BOTTOM OF THE CYLINDER AGAIN.

4 NOW THE EXHAUST VALVE OPENS.

THE PISTON MOVES UP THE CYLINDER AGAIN. THIS TIME IT PUSHES OUT THE EXHAUST GASES.

NOW THE PROCESS IS READY TO START AGAIN.

Electric Motor

An electric motor has a magnet inside and a piece of iron with wire wound round it, fixed to a shaft. When the motor is turned on, electricity flows through the wires.

The piece of iron becomes an electro-magnet. This spins round as the poles of the outside magnet attract and push away the poles of the electro-magnet.

When the electro-magnet has turned half way round, the electricity flows the other way. This changes the poles. So the shaft goes on turning.

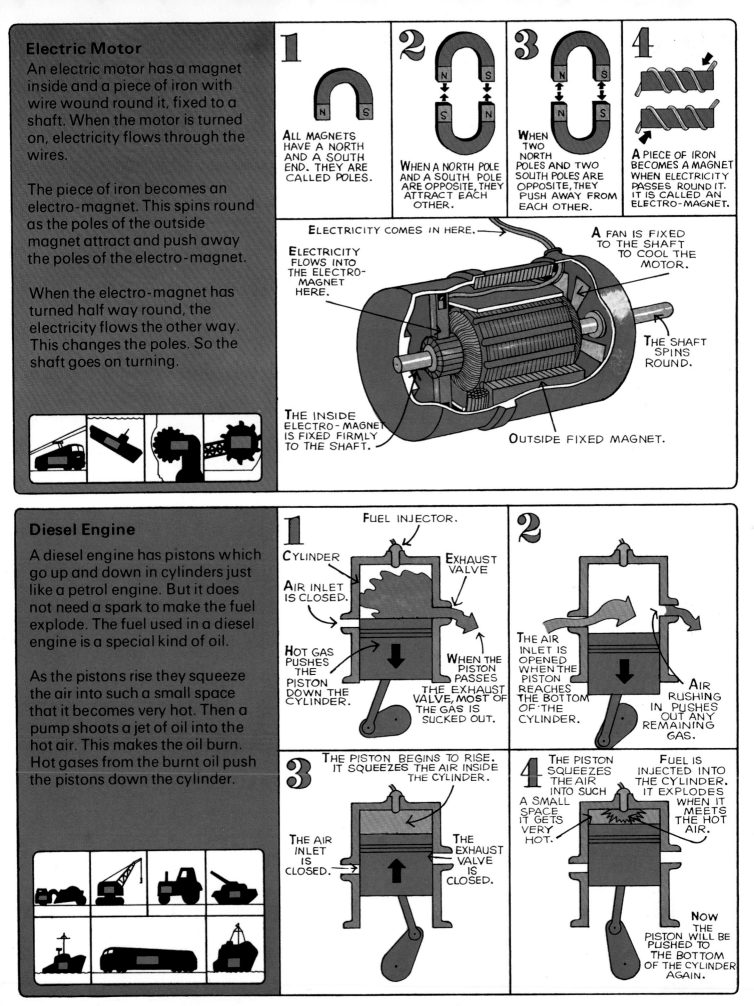

1 ALL MAGNETS HAVE A NORTH AND A SOUTH END. THEY ARE CALLED POLES.

2 WHEN A NORTH POLE AND A SOUTH POLE ARE OPPOSITE, THEY ATTRACT EACH OTHER.

3 WHEN TWO NORTH POLES AND TWO SOUTH POLES ARE OPPOSITE, THEY PUSH AWAY FROM EACH OTHER.

4 A PIECE OF IRON BECOMES A MAGNET WHEN ELECTRICITY PASSES ROUND IT. IT IS CALLED AN ELECTRO-MAGNET.

ELECTRICITY COMES IN HERE.

ELECTRICITY FLOWS INTO THE ELECTRO-MAGNET HERE.

A FAN IS FIXED TO THE SHAFT TO COOL THE MOTOR.

THE SHAFT SPINS ROUND.

THE INSIDE ELECTRO-MAGNET IS FIXED FIRMLY TO THE SHAFT.

OUTSIDE FIXED MAGNET.

Diesel Engine

A diesel engine has pistons which go up and down in cylinders just like a petrol engine. But it does not need a spark to make the fuel explode. The fuel used in a diesel engine is a special kind of oil.

As the pistons rise they squeeze the air into such a small space that it becomes very hot. Then a pump shoots a jet of oil into the hot air. This makes the oil burn. Hot gases from the burnt oil push the pistons down the cylinder.

1 FUEL INJECTOR. CYLINDER. AIR INLET IS CLOSED. EXHAUST VALVE. HOT GAS PUSHES THE PISTON DOWN THE CYLINDER. WHEN THE PISTON PASSES THE EXHAUST VALVE, MOST OF THE GAS IS SUCKED OUT.

2 THE AIR INLET IS OPENED WHEN THE PISTON REACHES THE BOTTOM OF THE CYLINDER. AIR RUSHING IN PUSHES OUT ANY REMAINING GAS.

3 THE PISTON BEGINS TO RISE. IT SQUEEZES THE AIR INSIDE THE CYLINDER. THE AIR INLET IS CLOSED. THE EXHAUST VALVE IS CLOSED.

4 THE PISTON SQUEEZES THE AIR INTO SUCH A SMALL SPACE IT GETS VERY HOT. FUEL IS INJECTED INTO THE CYLINDER. IT EXPLODES WHEN IT MEETS THE HOT AIR. NOW THE PISTON WILL BE PUSHED TO THE BOTTOM OF THE CYLINDER AGAIN.

Index

Aerial
  radio — 22
  television — 40
Aeroplanes
  Concorde — 6–7
  F.16 Fighter — 22–3
  Harrier — 10
  Hercules — 23
  mountain rescue — 27
  MRCA Fighter — 2
  reconnaissance SR. 71A — 2
After-burners — 6
Aircraft carrier — 24
Airport crash lorry — 26
Armoured car — 21
Asphalt — 30–1
Astronauts — 4–5
Autopilot — 25

Bathyscape — 19
Bow thrusters — 13
Building machines — 28–9
Bulldozers — 30

Camshaft — 44
Camouflage — 20–1
Coal-face cutter — 32
Combine harvester — 36–7
Concorde — 6–7
Concrete — 29, 31
Cranes — 12–13, 28–9, 34–5
Crankshaft — 44
Cylinder — 42–3, 44–5
Cars
  dragsters — 17
  racing — 16–17
  rally — 16

Dairy machines — 38–9
Diesel engines — 12, 14–15, 20–1, 26, 30–1, 36–7, 45
Dredging — 13
Drilling — 28, 34

Electricity — 14–15, 19, 34, 40, 44–5
Electric motors — 14–15, 18, 32, 33, 38–9, 41, 45
Electro-magnet — 45
Engines — 42–3, 44–5
Excavating — 30–1, 32–3

Farming
  combine harvesting — 36–7
  milking — 38–9
Firefighting — 26
Foundations — 28–30
Frigate — 24–5

Gases, exhaust — 10, 16, 25, 42–3, 44–5
Gas turbine engines — 9, 11, 24, 42
Gears — 15, 16
Gravity — 4

Helicopters — 11, 24, 35
Hovercraft — 8–9
Hydrofoil ship — 25

Jet aeroplanes — 7, 22–3
Jet engines — 7, 10, 23, 42

Kerosene — 42–3

Lavatory — 41
Lifeboats — 8, 12, 27

Mid-air refuelling — 10, 22
Milking — 38–9
Mining — 32–3
Missiles — 21, 23, 24–5
Motors — 42–3, 44–5

Oil rigs — 34–5
Oxygen — 4, 43

Pistons — 43, 44–5
Petrol engines — 16, 44

Racing
  car — 16–17
  dragster — 17
  motor cycle — 17
  power boat — 17
  rally car — 17
Radar — 7, 22, 24, 27
Refrigerator — 40
Rescue machines — 26–7
Rev counter — 17
Road-making machines — 30–1
Rocket motors — 43
Rudders — 7, 12

Satellite
  weather — 4
Ships
  aircraft carrier — 22
  container — 13
  dredger — 13
  frigate — 24–5
  hovercraft — 8–9
  hydrofoil — 24
  liner — 12–13
  log carrier — 12
  midget submarine — 18–19
  pipe-laying barge — 35
  submarine — 25
Snow blower — 26
Solar panels — 5
Sonar — 18–19
Spacecraft
  Apollo — 4–5
  Salyut — 5
  Soyuz — 5
  Viking — 4
Sparking plugs — 45
Steam engines — 14, 43
Steam turbines — 42
Steering
  aeroplanes — 6–7
  ships — 12–13
Swing wings — 22
Submarines
  midget — 18–19
  nuclear — 23

Tanks — 20–1
Telephone — 40
Television — 40
Torpedoes — 18
Tractors — 36, 37
Trains
  electric — 14–15
  goods — 15
  rack — 15
  steam — 14
  underground — 14
Transformer — 15
Turbo-jet engines — 6, 44
Tracks, crawler — 20, 30, 33

Underwater machines — 18–19

Warships — 24–5

Picture Index

The numbers show you the pages where you can find all these different machines.

Aeroplanes and Spacecraft

4	27	4	5	6,7	11	4,5

Ships and Submarines

12,13	27	13	12	8,9	18,19	19

Machines on Wheels

16,17	14	17	14	15	14,15	17

Fighting Machines

20,21	21	25	24,25	24	22	10

Working Machines

30,31	28	32,33	34,35	27	40	26
18	40	33	30,31	28,29	41	26
41	38,39	36,37	32	29	30	36,37

proost INTERNATIONAL BOOK PRODUCTION
PRINTED IN BELGIUM BY